CAN'T WE MAKE
MORAL JUDGEMENTS?

CAN'T WE MAKE
MORAL JUDGEMENTS?

Mary Midgley

St. Martin's Press
New York

First published in the United States of America in 1991

ISBN 0-312-06129-3 (cloth)

ISBN 0-312-08726-8 (paper)

Library of Congress Cataloging-in-Pubilcation Data

Midgley, Mary. 1919-
Can't we make moral judgements? / Mary Midgley.
       p. cm. — (Mind Matters)
   Inclues index.
   ISBN 0-312-06129-3
   1. Judgment (ethics) I. Title. II. Series.

BJ1408.5.M52 1991
1-70—dc20   90-26426
                            CIP

First Paperback Edition: February, 1993
10 9 8 7 6 5 4 3 2 1

CONTENTS

PREFACE

In the original preface to the "Mind Matters" series, I wrote: "Philosophers are very good at talking to one another. Some of them are also good at talking with other people... 'Mind Matters' is not 'Philosophy Made Easy' but rather 'Philosophy Made Intelligible' and the authors in this series have been chosen for more than their philosophical knowledge. Some of them are also experts in other fields such as medicine, computing or biology." The aim of the series was to open up philosophy to a wide general public by producing books which were clear, intelligible, meaningful and original and written in a lively and engaging manner. Pleasingly, the books have proved popular with a wide general readership and also are now used on a variety of university and college courses for lawyers, health workers, artists, teachers and computer scientists as well as for philosophers. Recent volumes continue to communicate philosophical ideas to all those who, for a great variety of reasons, find themselves questioning the foundations of their beliefs.

Each book begins with a perplexing question that we may ask ourselves without, perhaps, realising that we are "philosophizing": Do computers have minds? Can a pile of bricks be a work of art? Should we hold pathological killers responsible for their crimes? Such questions are considered and new questions raised with frequent reference to the views of major philosophers. The authors go further than this, however. It is not their intention to produce a potted history of philosophical ideas. They also make their own contributions to the subject, suggesting different avenues of thought to explore. The result is a collection of original writings on a wide range of topics produced for all those who find philosophy as fascinating and compelling as they do.

Mary Midgley has a well-earned reputation as a philosopher who knows and cares about important issues in the real world. Through her newspaper column, her frequent broadcasts and her involvement with environmental and animal protection groups, she has become as well-known outside the philosophical world as she is within it. In this lively and approachable discussion Mary Midgley turns a spotlight on the fashionable view that moral judgements are something we no longer need or use. Guiding the reader through the diverse approaches to this complex subject, she points out the strong, confident beliefs about such things as the value of freedom that underlie our supposed scepticism about values. She knows how the question of whether or not we can make moral judgements must inevitably affect our attitudes not only to the law and its institutions, but also to events that occur in our daily lives, and suggests that mistrust of moral judgement may be making life even harder for us than it would be otherwise.

INTRODUCTION

This little book attacks certain difficulties that seem to get in the way of all of us today when we try to think about moral problems—certain highly confusing doubts about the possibility of thinking morally at all. The book does not presuppose any acquaintance with philosophy. It is not intended, either, as a general introduction to existing moral philosophy, still less to any particular disputes that are currently going on about it. It is meant to be something more like a map of the problems—many of them timeless, others sharply contemporary—which face us all today when we try to sort out moral questions. It covers the confusing terrain in which we seem to get lost before we can come to grips with the main issues. It tries to suggest possible routes through that waste land.

I certainly hope that it can also serve as an "introduction to philosophy" in the sense that it may light up for some of its readers both the exciting nature of philosophical questions and the possibility of dealing with them effectively. (I believe that the kind of fatalistic despair which is often preached about that possibility is mistaken.) Though there is nothing technical in this book, I have freely discussed in it certain large-scale philosophical views that are crucial to its topic. Since these are part of a general structure shaping our thought, I hope that many readers will find it worth their while to trace them further. Like plumbing and electric cables, philosophy underlies much more of our lives than we notice—in fact, it is simply the study of the wide, unnoticed thought-patterns that do so. Finding out a bit more about these can often be uncommonly useful.

The book owes a great deal to what I have been taught over many years by my students in the Department of Philosophy at the University of Newcastle on Tyne—a very good department which, like too many others, has now been closed to save money. I found that those students, who were often sharp, lively people, and extremely keen to investigate the subject they had chosen, seemed to experience, on top of the difficulties that were part of that subject, certain others which did not seem so necessary.

These difficulties interested me very much, and, in thinking about them over the years, I realised how widespread they are. I have come to believe they are very important. Some of these difficulties have indeed received a good deal of philosophical attention in recent times, and the academic tradition is certainly expanding itself in the direction of dealing with them. The ideas that can be found in Wittgenstein's later writings are very helpful here. I believe, however, that these matters still deserve much more serious philosophical attention. And, since it is not very easy to read Wittgenstein, they certainly need more widespread discussion.

I would like to thank my colleagues at Newcastle, especially Judith Hughes and Michael Bavidge, and many elsewhere, notably Timothy Sprigge and Brenda Almond, for helpful suggestions. Geoffrey and David Midgley have given me an enormous amount of help. But again, the main debt I owe is to that long succession of students. Above all, perhaps, I owe it to the one (now nameless) who made, long ago, the indispensable remark with which I start my first chapter.

CAN'T WE MAKE
MORAL JUDGEMENTS?

1

Can We Base Freedom on Ignorance?

THE PARADOX

"But surely it's always wrong to make moral judgements?"

This is the manifesto that I once heard someone lay down in an argument about the duty of toleration. It was spoken ardently and confidently, with no expectation that it might be questioned. It was not said as a new discovery, but as a moral platitude, something so obvious that it need only be mentioned to be accepted. And the speaker was not being at all eccentric in so pronouncing it; this confidence is normal today. In the last few decades, the word "judgemental" has been specially coined and is used, along with the slightly older word "moralistic", to describe and attack this particular form of wrongdoing.

The question is: is this manifesto itself a moral judgement, or not? At first glance, to say that anything is wrong surely does seem to be a moral judgement. Remarks like this are in fact used to express active disapproval of particular people who are considered *guilty* of judging, to blame these people, to stigmatise them, to discourage them from doing it again and to discourage others from imitating them. These are surely characteristic uses of moral judgement.

Of course, people talking like this might not mean to give the manifesto so strong a meaning. They might mean by "a moral judgement" something narrower and more obviously wrong. They might merely mean poking your nose into other people's affairs or forming crude opinions about things that you don't understand, and expressing them offensively. If that were all, then "being judgemental" would simply be a new name for being

a busybody and a nosey-parker. Or again, they might have in mind chiefly
the fact that blame can lead to punishment, and that terrible crimes have
been committed, in all ages, under the pretext of punishment. But to make
a moral judgement is not the same thing as to punish. If that were all, they
should surely be talking about punishment itself.

Clearly, these weaker meanings are not all that is involved. If they had
been, the new label "being judgemental" would not have been invented.
What the statement attacks is not just the intrusive expression of opinions
about other people, nor any possible vindictive action on those opinions
afterwards, but the forming of opinions in the first place. The ban is on
judging —not only on judging in a court of law, where sentence and
punishment may follow, but in ordinary life. And the reason given for this
ban concerns our powers of judgement. It denies that we are in a position
to decide these moral questions even in our own minds.

That is why ambitious talk of judgement has displaced humbler traditional accusations such as vindictiveness or nosey-parkerdom. The old
moral objection to intrusive *conduct* is of course still there, but it is now
backed by the new philosophical ruling that nothing at all can be known
in the sphere of morals. If that is right, then the objection of vindictive
punishment is not being made as a moral objection; it is a logical one. It
simply springs from the impossibility of judging that anything is a crime.
A direct moral objection to brutal punishment would itself be just one
more moral judgement, and it would not be sustainable if the general
invalidation of all moral judgement works.

If it does work, then moral questions are (as is often said) just a matter
of everybody's own subjective opinion, of their taste. In the terms of this
hypothesis people can no more "impose judgements" on one another here
than they can impose their own taste in clothes or food. This seems to
mean that moral judgements are not really in any ordinary sense judgements at all. "Making judgements" in this sphere is not so much wrong as
impossible. The veto on doing it is something like the veto on witchcraft:
it forbids us to pretend to do something which in fact cannot be done.

HIGH-MINDED SCEPTICISM

In theory, a rather general scepticism of this kind is common today. But
"being sceptical" can mean two very different things. It can mean habitually

asking questions, or it can mean being so sure that there are no answers that one simply issues denials instead. These two approaches may be called enquiring and dogmatic scepticism. It is the second kind to which I want to draw attention. Throughout many contemporary discussions of moral questions in the social sciences it is assumed that these questions make no sense, that there can be no rational way to answer them. Thus, the distinguished and humane penologist Baroness Wootton, resisting the suggestion that there might be some real connection between the concepts of crime and sin, wrote as follows:

> Can we then in the modern world identify a class of inherently wicked actions? Lord Devlin, who has returned more than once to this theme, holds that we still can ... nevertheless, this attempt to revive the lawyer's distinction between ... things which are bad in themselves and things which are merely prohibited ... cannot, I think, succeed. In the first place, the statement that a real crime is one about which the good citizen would feel guilty is surely circular. For how is the good citizen to be defined in this context unless as one who feels guilty about committing the crimes that Lord Devlin would classify as "real"?
>
> (Barbara Wootton, 1981, p. 42)

According to this view, there are no actions bad in themselves and no citizens good in themselves; there are only ones that Lord Devlin (or someone else) might think good or bad. If we want to say that rape and murder and child-abuse are terrible crimes while parking offences are not, that is just our personal preference and we can give no rational ground for it.

Again, arguing that the treatment of offenders ought to depend simply on predictions about how this treatment would affect the particular offender, not on judgements about the gravity of the offence committed, Baroness Wootton writes:

> ... Although prediction techniques are still not as reliable as could be wished, they are at least open to objective testing, which should provide data by which their reliability may reasonably be expected to improve, whereas the validity of moral evaluations of the relative wickedness of different criminal acts is merely a matter of opinion and cannot in the nature of the case ever be subjected to any objective test.
>
> (Barbara Wootton, 1981, p. 63)

PROBLEMS OF FALSE UNIVERSALITY

These remarks have a characteristic that we shall find repeatedly in others like them. They were actually aimed at quite a narrow application to particular issues in penal reform. And the moral attitudes that called for them on those particular issues were (as most of us might suppose) admirable. But they were so sweepingly expressed that, if they are taken literally, they carry a much wider and more destructive message. It is a message of radical disbelief in the whole existing system of values, including the conceptions of humaneness and regard for the common good which were obviously central to the writer.

Baroness Wootton certainly did not see the importance of these ideals as a mere "matter of opinion" in the sense which that phrase usually bears—namely, either as a trivial matter of taste, or as really dubious. (For instance, if one were not quite sure about the importance of the common good, one would scarcely be likely to go to the fearful trouble of campaigning for penal reform.) What is actually involved in calling something a "matter of opinion" is a point to be considered later. But the strength of this writer's objections to the notion of retributive punishment—objections that were certainly moral as well as prudential—led her to use a far more drastic language than was needed for her thought, or than she would have consented to see embodied in practice.

For instance, if one really allotted punishments merely by their probable effect on those punished, without any reference to the offences committed, there would, it seems, be no need to wait for any offence to be committed. People who seemed likely to be dangerous could simply be taken into care and given whatever treatment seemed likely to improve their conduct, without the need to wait until they committed an actual offence. (This could, of course, happen to any of us, since we are all imperfect and most of us are capable of improvement.) And since reward as well as punishment currently works on retributive principles, it too would have to be reorganised in the same way. Honours and favours should be handed out, not to those who had earned them, but to those selected as likely to respond best to incentives.

This misleading appearance of universality has been common in such theoretical discourses. Probably there is as much of it in the less formal, more everyday kinds of dogmatic moral scepticism that have become even more familiar. Here are three examples from a recent detective story by P.D. James:

(1) Hilary has been making what she feels to be a justified claim on Alex:

> After she had finished speaking he said quietly, "That sounds like an ultimatum."
>
> "I wouldn't call it that."
>
> "What would you call it then, blackmail?"
>
> "After what's happened between us? I'd call it justice."
>
> "Let's stick to ultimatum. Justice is too grandiose a concept for the commerce between us two."
>
> (P.D. James, 1989, p. 139)

(2) Caroline has been pressing Jonathan to lie to the police so as to give her a false alibi for the murder, but he refuses. Contemptuously, she drops her request:

> "All right!" [she says] "I'm asking too much. I know how you feel about truth, honesty, your boy-scout Christianity. I'm asking you to sacrifice your good opinion of yourself. No one likes doing that. We all need our self-esteem. . ."
>
> (P.D. James, 1989, p. 187)

In the third, Alice, the actual murderess (seen throughout as a sympathetic, though damaged character) is explaining to her friend Meg why she did the murder. Meg protests:

> "Nothing Hilary Roberts did deserved death."
>
> "I'm not arguing that she deserved to die. It doesn't matter whether she was happy, or childless, or even much use to anybody but herself. What I'm saying is that I wanted her dead."
>
> "That seems to me so evil that it's beyond my understanding. Alice, what you did was a dreadful sin."
>
> Alice laughed. The sound was so full-throated, almost happy, as if the amusement were genuine. "Meg, you continue to astonish me. You use words which are no longer in the general vocabulary, not even in the Church's, so

I'm told. The implications of that simple little word are beyond my comprehension."

(P.D. James, 1989, p. 388)

The same device recurs often in the conversation in this novel (and in many others), with this same implication that the moral language other people speak is a foreign one, something "no longer in the general vocabulary"—a language that the more sophisticated speaker finds senseless, childish, naive and (most damning of all) out of fashion. Since it is always unnerving to be sneered at, this tactic is often successful in silencing people, both in fiction and real life. But that is quite another thing from saying that it makes sense.

Virtually always, the sense of the tactic is annulled by its context. Again, there is false universality. The characters who talk like this are in general quite as ready as other people to live most of their lives by existing standards, to pass judgements about others, and to invoke morality where it happens to be on their side. They still feel high-minded, and this is not an accident, but a necessary consequence of their wish to be seen as reformers. They are "immoralists" in the sense that they want to back and recommend actions currently taken to be immoral. But this backing and recommending is itself unavoidably a moral stand. It is not possible to sneer at other people's standards without committing yourself to rival standards of your own.

Nietzsche, who patented the word immoralist, spent a great deal of his time protesting in this way against current standards by recommending different ones. He also tried, and sometimes very seriously, to get rid of the notion of moral standards altogether. The word "amoralist" has since been coined to name this more radical campaign. However, it faces serious difficulties, which will occupy us a good deal in this book.

In P.D. James's novel, both Alex and Caroline are noticeably self-righteous people, contemptuous of others. Caroline in particular habitually shows priggish contempt for people whom she thinks lacking in quite traditional values such as courage and honesty. Moreover she at once goes on to appeal—successfully—to Jonathan's sympathy and consideration to make him lie for her, which he would scarcely have done if he had accepted the amoralist manifesto she has just pronounced. Again, the murder Alice commits is altruistic, indeed, by her account to Meg, quite incredibly high-principled. I have the impression that P.D. James takes these amoralist manifestos fairly seriously, and that she is anxious to get them a serious hearing by showing the people who speak them as honourable and high-principled characters. The trouble is that this only suggests that they can't mean exactly what they say.

Tom Stoppard puts this point sharply at the end of his play *Professional Foul*, where two philosophers are returning by air from an Ethics Congress in Prague. McKendrick, the younger, who has been advancing some dramatic amoralist views about the flexibility of moral principles, is rather surprised to find that his fuddy-duddy companion has managed to smuggle something out at the airport:

McKendrick. What was it?

Anderson. A thesis. Apparently rather slanderous from the State's point of view.

McKendrick. Where did you hide it?

Anderson. In your briefcase. *(Pause)*

McKendrick. You what?

Anderson. Last night. I'm afraid I reversed a principle. *(McKendrick opens his briefcase and finds Hollar's envelope. Anderson takes it from him. McKendrick is furious)*

McKendrick. You utter bastard!

Anderson. I thought you would approve.

McKendrick. Don't get clever with me. *(He relapses, shaking.)* Jesus. It's not quite playing the game, is it?

Anderson. No. I suppose not. But they were very unlikely to search *you*.

McKendrick. That's not the bloody point.

Anderson. I thought it was. But you could be right. Ethics is a very complicated business. That's why we have these congresses.

(Tom Stoppard, 1978, p.179)

DIFFICULTIES OF THE EXTRA-TERRESTRIAL POSITION

The point I am making here is not just a petty one, about chance inconsistencies of particular characters or particular authors. It is a point about the sheer size of morality. People who talk about opting out of it are thinking of it as a mere local set of restrictions—often sexual restrictions—something comparable to a district one might leave, or a set of by-laws that one might repeal or decide to ignore. But in fact this community of standards and ideals is something much wider, much more pervasive, more enclosing—much more like the air we breathe. It is not even comparable with a particular language that we might decide to stop speaking, though that could itself be traumatic enough. It is more like the condition of speaking—and thinking—in any language at all.

Getting right outside morality would be rather like getting outside the atmosphere. It would mean losing the basic social network within which we live and communicate with others, including all those others in the past who have formed our culture. If we can imagine this deprived state at all, it would be a solitary condition close to that of autism or extreme depression—a state where, although intelligence can still function, there is no sense of community with others, no shared wishes, principles, aspirations or ideals, no mutual trust or fellowship with those outside, no preferred set of concepts, nothing agreed on as important.

People whom we sometimes call amoral are not actually in this extra-terrestrial condition. They are merely using standards somewhat different from our own. Their distinctiveness often looks much greater than it is, because a shared moral background is so important to us that even quite a slight difference of standards—even a small shift of emphasis—can make an impression of great strangeness. Sometimes it is refreshing, making change and development possible. But just as often it causes alarm and gives both sides the impression that they are divided by something as vast as the difference between being inside and outside morality.

The charge of senselessness which Alice brings is often used to express this sense of shock. "I simply can't understand it," we complain, and this remark is well known to count, not as a request for explanation, but as a serious criticism, sometimes a declaration of war. Reformers who want to stress individual liberty have therefore often accepted and returned this incredulous repudiation, and have claimed to be what other people have called them—outside morality. But this no more has to be literally true than most of the other wild claims that are generated in controversy.

NOTES

Lord Devlin, a distinguished judge, had argued in an interesting book (*The Enforcement of Morals*, Oxford University Press, 1965) that every society must be committed to some morality in order to exist at all, and that laws were quite properly not just regulations for convenience, but also expressions of that morality. Unfortunately, because the views he expressed about the particular form that our morality should now take struck many people as narrow and unimaginative, the force of his general position did not get the attention that perhaps it should have done.

Works quoted in this chapter:

Baroness Wootton, Barbara, *Crime and the Criminal Law* (London, Stevens, 1981) pp. 42, 63

P.D. James, *Devices and Desires* (London, Faber and Faber, 1989) pp. 139, 187, 388

Tom Stoppard, *Professional Foul* (London, Faber and Faber, published 1984 in a collection with *Squaring the Circle* and *Every Good Boy Deserves Favour*) p. 179

2

Starting from Where We Are

UNPACKING THE PARCEL

It should be becoming clear that the moral scepticism, the incredulity about all moral judgements that I am talking of is not a simple thing, but a whole complex of varying attitudes. As we unpack it, we shall find many different elements in it, among them some of great value. But we shall find great difficulty in making sense of it as a single whole.

It may seem rather confusing to open the subject at this everyday level, by starting from extreme, everyday pronouncements and pointing out the clashes between what they seem to say and the intentions of the people who make them. I have chosen to do this because I think it is often easier to understand current confusions by starting from the familiar forms in which they are expressed in our own lives than by using the less familiar, more carefully guarded formulations of moral theorists. Besides, it is the ideas we actually live by that we most need to understand.

I think it is important to notice how very *negative* these everyday manifestos are. It is much clearer what they are attacking than why they are attacking it and what they are proposing instead. On these points they vary enormously, which is why I am stressing the false universality that conceals their differences.

This approach from the confusions of everyday thought does not at all mean that I simply want to shoot down the whole attitude behind the incomplete statements. The difficulties about moral judgement are real. They are not due to chance pieces of incompetence on the part of people who discuss this sort of thing. They spring from major value-conflicts— clashes and gaps between the various ideals and principles we live by—

which are deeply rooted in our culture today and affect us all. Indeed, more generally, it is hardly ever sensible to refute any argument just by pointing out an inconsistency within it. What is needed is to trace the considerations on both sides that have led us to hold clashing views, and to rethink them somehow so as to do justice to all these elements.

THE INDIGNANT REFORMERS

We must start by looking more fully at the context in which this sort of conflict arises, before turning to the small print of the arguments that are used. A very important point about that context is surely the one already touched on—that explicit, sceptical attacks on moral judgement are not usually made (as we might perhaps expect) by lotus-eating cynics anxious to save themselves the trouble of thinking whether anything is right or wrong at all. (These people seldom bother with argument.) Often, as we have seen, anti-judgementalists are people seriously concerned to protect the victims of moral intrusion. Often, too, they are thinkers concerned about the value of the inner life—eager to save us from spoiling our lives by imposing mistaken moral standards on ourselves. Again, they sometimes want education changed and society reshaped in a way that will make this kind of inner oppression less likely.

Both these last kinds of consideration were very powerful with Nietzsche, which is why, though he called himself an "immoralist", he was also in a very important sense a moralist. He desperately wanted to change the world; he was thoroughly confident that the changes he proposed were the right ones, and the chief tool that he used to promote these changes was not hesitation or doubt but burning moral indignation. Nietzsche's views will be discussed more fully in chapter 13.

ARE AMORALISTS MORALISTS?

Thus the campaign against "moral judgement" seems often to spring from, and to rely on, strong and confidently held moral positions—decisions both about what is important and about the way in which these important things should be changed, or not changed. All these positions, if taken seriously, have clear and specific implications about what actually ought and ought not to be done. The question then is what is the standing of these new, innovative judgements? Are they armoured in some way against the sceptical solvent that is invoked to destroy all the others? Or are they perhaps not to be classed as moral judgements at all?

THE BACKGROUND: WHY FREEDOM MATTERS

Before plunging into detailed discussion of this, it may be helpful to sketch hastily what I think our main difficulty is—to outline briefly the range of topics that we must later go into more fully.

In our history, two quite different moral insights seem to have become entangled, forming a plausible argument which in our time has so dazzled people that it has seemed to transform the whole moral scene. One is a tremendous exaltation of individual freedom. The other is a sceptical or incredulous approach to knowledge, designed to weed out all inadequate forms of it in order to make room for modern science. Both these insights stem from the Enlightenment, and both are still extremely powerful in our lives.

These two ideas have been combined to form the claim that respect for freedom is founded on people's ignorance of each other. On this principle, the reason why we ought to leave other people free is simply that we do not know anything about them which could justify us in interfering. The formula of freedom is then close to our manifesto, and runs something like this: it is always wrong to interfere with other people's actions, because we can never know that any action is wrong.

Until you notice the internal conflict in it, this formula seems to resolve at one stroke two very difficult and disturbing questions. The first is: why is freedom so important? This is a pressing question because freedom does sometimes clash with other ideals, and when it does, we need to know whether it ought to prevail. The second is about the standing of non-scientific reasoning generally. In an age where science reigns, what sort of validity can non-scientific forms of thought, including moral judgement, possibly have? Puzzled people have hoped to have found an answer to the first question by simply answering "none" to the second. Freedom then becomes the supreme value; it has to be infinite because nobody ever knows enough to be in a position to restrict it.

This rum solution involves some obvious confusions. It looks attractive because there is a range of important cases where our ignorance of other people's lives and standards actually does provide a good reason for not interfering with them. These cases arise especially between groups with different customs, such as different classes or cultures, and they can be disastrous politically where one group is trying to rule the other. Thus imperialist powers have often done great harm by putting down religious or marital customs that they simply did not understand.

But could there be reason to suggest that this ignorance—so obvious in particular situations—is something which extends over the whole field of morality? Are we just as ignorant about more familiar matters, where we seem to know so much more? And even if we are indeed so ignorant, can this ignorance possibly be the *only* reason, or even the main reason, why we ought to respect freedom?

Ignorance, after all, provides only a reason for *indifference*, for detachment, for not caring about what other people do or suffer. That is the attitude we might have to have towards alien beings if a set of them came to live somewhere on earth, and were so totally incomprehensible to us that we could form no opinion at all about what they did or suffered. That indifference would indeed often stop us interfering with them. But it is hard to imagine a detachment so total, so far beyond the range of anything attempted in science fiction. And it is not an attitude that we could possibly take for our social relations with those around us.

Ignorance plainly is not the kind of reason that we normally have in mind when we say that we should respect other people's freedom. The reasons why we respect it are different and much more positive. They arise out of the fact that we honour and trust other people, that we think them capable of acting independently, and that we believe independent, self-chosen action to have in general a special kind of value.

This last belief is another characteristic contribution of modern Enlightenment thought, placing a special value on spontaneous action that flows from personal decision, as opposed to the same acts done automatically or under pressure. As John Stuart Mill put it:

> It really is of importance, not only what men do, but also what manner of men they are that do it. . . Supposing it were possible to get houses built, corn grown, battles fought, causes tried, and even churches erected and prayers said, by machinery—by automatons in human form—it would be a considerable loss to exchange for these automatons even the men and women

who at present inhabit the more civilized parts of the world, and who assuredly are but starved specimens of what nature can and will produce.

(Mill, 1936, p. 117)

This strong, positive moral judgement—now so familiar and acceptable to most of us—explains the reason why we should respect the freedom, not only of those about whom we are ignorant, but also of the people we know well. It operates too, not only where we think we cannot judge the rightness or wrongness of their actions, but also where we think we can judge it, and have judged that these actions are not wrong. (That, too, is of course a moral judgement.) This seems to be the position, for instance, over the justification of homosexual activity, or of different ways of educating children, and it is what distinguishes these cases from a justification of murder. When we do think other people's actions wrong— for instance in cases such as murder or child abuse—we do not usually believe that we ought not to interfere. Of course the borderlines between these two kinds of cases are misty, raising large issues which must be discussed in the next chapters. Toleration is a complex issue. But virtually nobody thinks it our duty to tolerate every kind of conduct in others.

SORTING OUT THE MORAL ISSUES

What we mainly need to notice here is that this exaltation of individual freedom apparently *is itself a moral judgement*, and that the arguments supporting it are moral arguments. This is as true of the principles requiring respect for freedom as it is of other principles equally fundamental to our life today, for instance: that it is wrong to punish people by burning them to death, however gravely they may have offended. When propositions like these are questioned, we support them by moral arguments. It is crucial to distinguish these arguments from epistemological ones—arguments about how much we know and what our knowledge amounts to—which are the other main set we have to deal with in this book. When we come to discuss these other questions about knowledge, in chapters 3 and 17, we will deal more fully both with the nature of moral judgements and the kinds of reason that can be given for them.

THE NEUTRALITY OF EXAMPLES

A brief note seems needed here about the examples we must use. Throughout this discussion, I shall often have to mention particular moral judgements simply as examples, without going at any length into the arguments for or against them. These will as far as possible be ones that many readers are likely to hold already, and which are often combined with the anti-judgemental stance from which we started. But since what we are discussing is the validity of moral judgements in general, readers who disagree with these particular judgements need only substitute for them different ones—perhaps indeed opposite ones—that they do accept. The point is simply to examine the way in which moral judgement of some kind is a necessary element in our thinking.

NOTES

Works quoted in this chapter:

John Stuart Mill, "On Liberty" (1859) in *Utilitarianism, Liberty and Representative Government* (Everyman Edition, London, Dent and Dutton, 1936, p. 117.) Further quotations from this essay will be marked simply *Liberty*.

3

Why There Is Trouble Over Knowledge

SCEPTICISM AND THE QUEST FOR SAFETY

Knowledge is now an awkward topic, but it is not one we can avoid. The trouble is that, since the 16th century, the standards by which we in the West judge knowledge have risen enormously, making it look doubtful whether we know things about which people used to be perfectly confident. The dawn of modern science was accompanied by an intense, genuinely enquiring scepticism because it involved a quest for a new kind of certainty—for guarantees of security in knowledge of a kind no other culture has ever looked for. This did involve raising the standards of evidence required for the answers, and therefore rejecting many that had formerly been accepted. Descartes, the 17th-century philosopher who chiefly shaped this movement, instituted his systematic doubt—a relentless sifting of the credentials of all kinds of knowledge—in order to make possible this quest for absolute scientific certainty.

That quest has of course produced amazing successes. But as we travel on further, questions begin to arise about how far this search for certainty can be carried, and about just what it means. What, eventually, is the point of it?

It has become plain that we cannot produce the absolute finality in knowledge that the pioneers hoped for—a set of scientific theories that will need never to be altered. Both Newton's physics and Euclid's geometry seemed at first to have this final, infallible status, but both have proved not to have it. They have not, of course, been disproved, but they have turned out to be only partial truths applying in limited areas and needing restatement to explain their position. They are not the all-embracing finalities that they once seemed.

FOUNDATION TROUBLE

Along with this change, the idea that these theories—or any others—could be used as *foundations* for all knowledge—placed at the bottom of the pile and logically supporting all other knowledge—no longer looks plausible. The general progress of science looks less and less like the piling of bricks into a pre-set pattern, or a journey to a pre-set final goal. It looks more and more like a cumulative, living enterprise, perhaps an ongoing journey where different challenges will always call for fresh responses—where indeed much is learned—but the solving of one problem always raises others which are different and will need new approaches.

It is important that this is not a tragic or discouraging conclusion. It should surely make us suspect that the goal of secure finality was not the right one in the first place. Of course Renaissance scientists were quite right to insist on greater accuracy, precision and thoroughness of method. But these are not all that is needed for a successful enquiry.

There is also the matter of finding the right question. Some questions are trivial; pursuing them by the best methods in the world will not yield answers worth having. Other questions are demonstrably important, and it is worth our while to pursue them even when we are not at all sure that we have yet found the right methods for doing it.

Finding the right questions, and then finding suitable methods for answering them, are tricky enterprises. For both of them various arts—various sets of known skills—do exist, but these arts are not sciences. They are fluid, always growing, and not the kind of thing that could ever be fully formalised. This means that the pattern for the development of thought which seemed so plausible from the 16th century to the 19th has proved to need alteration. The building metaphor has begun to look thoroughly unsuitable. Instead of starting by laying down what seemed capable of being finalised—physics and mathematics—and then piling up the rest of knowledge in a skyscraper of rocklike finality, we are now beginning to see our knowledge as something more like a set of maps of an ever-changing and ever-expanding territory. Instead of trying to make sure that the map is secure and final, we now see the need to pay more attention to filling in the enormous gaps in it—to making it reasonably comprehensive. Would you rather travel with a map that was guaranteed infallible, but that only showed certain isolated patches, or with one that showed the general shape of the country, and gave quite a lot of detail, but warned you that it might contain some mistakes? If we hesitate at this choice, we should perhaps remember that the guarantee of infallibility has not proved to be worth much in any case.

THE PROBLEM OF SAFETY

It also seems interesting to ask: was the ideal of finality a reasonable one anyway? The absolute certainty that was aimed at was a form of safety, of security, and it may be worth while to think about ideals of this kind. When we try to make something safer—roads or medicines or swimming-baths—we have before us the ultimate aim of removing all danger, and this can be extremely helpful in making us persistent. All the same, the time comes when this aim conflicts with others that we think more important. A swimming-bath in which diving is forbidden because it is all too shallow to dive in, where lifebelts must always be worn and which is only open on alternate Thursdays when the safety-officer can be present, is not a satisfactory swimming-bath. Similarly, a standard of knowledge that only approves enquiries where the familiar methods of physical science can be used is, for many of the purposes of our thought, an unusable standard.

WHAT IS SCIENTIFIC?

During the 20th century, however, this kind of standard has been widely applied, and the suspicion of being "unscientific" has been thrown on many perfectly respectable kinds of enquiry. There is a confusion in this suspicion because the words "science" and "scientific" were used, until the mid-19th century, for any systematic enquiry. Only at that time did they begin to be confined to the physical sciences. This had the unfortunate effect of making it seem that what was not physical science could not be systematic at all.

This suspicion was cast on a great many other departments of thought besides the moral judgements (and value-judgements generally) that are our present business. Historical and geographical knowledge was also attacked as "unscientific" because it deals in particular facts and provisional generalisations rather than in universal laws, and because not much of it is mathematical. Many branches of biology, too, got marked down as not yet being "exact sciences". Studies such as linguistics, law and logic, when mentioned, were also observed not to be much like physics.

But worse still, the certainties of daily life—the evidence of our senses, of our memory and of testimony from those around us, sources on which all our more technical information depends —are certainly not gained through anything called "the scientific method". They are rather quarries that supply the raw material on which scientific methods must work, and if they are uncertain, the science itself is uncertain too. Even in mathematics, disputes abound and time-honoured certainties can be upset, as happened with the discovery of non-Euclidean geometries in the last century. There is therefore a vast spread of essential knowledge that forms no part of "science" even in the broadest sense and cannot be supported by it. Among that spread of non-scientific thought, moral judgements, and other value-judgements such as aesthetic ones, certainly do take their place somewhere. To say that is not to locate them in some limbo of irrationality. It is simply to say that they are not part of *science*, any more than science is part of history.

All this (again) is not a disaster. It simply shows that we should get rid of some unreal expectations. There is no single, infallible form of knowledge, forming a standard against which all others must be measured and by whose help they will all finally be made impregnable. Instead, there are many different ways of knowing, each with their own standards and their own suitable kinds of evidence. None of them is infallible, but all can be made more—or less—reliable by suitable treatment. The pattern of our knowledge is much more like that of a forest of different interdependent plants, or a city of different interconnected buildings, than of a single enormous building piled on a single foundation-stone.

MANY KINDS OF KNOWLEDGE

This does not make our knowledge any less secure, though it does make it less simple. The way in which we know historical facts—say about things like the Industrial Revolution, or geographical ones about things like the composition of the Andes—is quite different from the way in which we know the general rules about the behaviour of gases, but it is not "less scientific" in the sense of being any less systematic or less reliable. Different again are the ways in which a pianist knows the "Appassionata", or the way in which we can know French, or know the South Coast, or know the nine times table, or know *Lycidas* by heart, or know our way home. Moreover we also know people, and recognise definite ways of knowing them more or less well. (It is interesting to ask what we mean by saying "Oh I couldn't ask him that—I don't know him well enough. . . ")

Many kinds of knowledge are ways of "knowing how" to act and think rather than of "knowing that" something is true. They are skills and acquired capacities rather than propositions. But they are still kinds of knowledge. And indeed it is not much use to "know propositions"— merely to know them by heart, or to possess information—if you do not also know how to think about them. The word "know" is, by origin, closely connected with the word "can", and many of its important senses still keep that link.

WHERE WOULD MORALITY COME IN?

Just supposing (for we must take the possibility seriously) that it *is* sometimes possible to know whether something is right or wrong, where would we expect that piece of knowledge to figure among this range of skills and capacities? Gilbert Ryle brought out the interesting way in which it differs from an ordinary typical fact-finding in an article called "On Forgetting the Difference Between Right and Wrong". It would be very odd (Ryle suggested) to talk of forgetting *that* difference, though one could perfectly well forget factual differences, such as that between the chemistry of wasp-stings and bee-stings, or between Hungary and Romania. Perhaps (he suggested) knowing the difference between right and wrong might be more like knowing how to swim or how to ride a bicycle. These skills are not vague or woolly. They are precise and highly differentiated, but they are inarticulate and quite deeply worked into our muscles. But in the case of right and wrong it might not be so much our muscles that are involved as our large-scale cognitive and practical attitudes—our whole policies for thinking and living, our ways of relating to those around us.

Because our tradition, following Descartes, has drawn such a firm line between scientific knowledge and all the rest of our mental life, we now find it quite hard to attend clearly to the wide spectrum of territory that Ryle mentioned, intermediate between that narrow kind of knowledge and pure, uncriticised emotion or pure unreflective action. We must surely, however, attend sharply to this territory if we want to understand the paradoxes of moral judgement. We shall notice a number of quite well-organised ways of thinking which are certainly not science, but are equally certainly not just mindless feelings or habits or urges or reflexes or automatic reactions. It is among these that we shall probably need to look for a suitable place for moral reflection.

HOW DO WE DECIDE ABOUT FACTS?

One more example of these organised, but not fully formalised, ways of thinking is probably worth mentioning here, just to lay the suspicion that they are all really no more than a slosh of formless, uncriticisable emotional reactions. That example concerns *factual* judgement—the set of skills by which we assess evidence and decide whether particular propositions are true or false. This is often quite difficult. There are skills involved here; some people know how to make these judgements better than others. But these skills cannot themselves be reduced to a set of propositions and written down in a book. (If they could, making the judgements would be much easier than it is.)

Certainly, there are many aspects of the art of judging which can be explained and written down, and the whole business of making such decisions is much more fully articulated than the business of swimming or riding a bicycle. But these guidelines necessarily involve standards, and standards are not themselves facts. Moreover, the guidelines only take us so far into the business of judging, and even where they have been most fully and carefully written out—for instance in lawcourts or in the sciences themselves—there is notoriously still room for constant doubts and disputes. (The notion of science itself as being dispute-free is of course as comical as the notion that law can be so, but it does sometimes seem to lie behind arguments of this kind.) The art of thinking is something much larger, much more active and more complex than a mere battery of facts and printed guidelines.

Here, too, it is interesting to raise the question whether somebody could manage to *forget* the difference between truth and falsehood? To bring this about, we would surely need to imagine a fairly extreme case of demoralisation—perhaps the state that might be produced by prolonged, habitual and indiscriminate lying, or a kind of depression where all questions had ceased to matter? That would mean that the whole apparatus of thought had become disorganised; its processes could no longer work because its normal aims had been lost. It could not be just a matter of forgetting a particular fact like the difference between wasp-stings and bee-stings. It would be more like losing one's whole power of factual reasoning. To be *demoralised* is to be utterly lost.

WHAT JUDGEMENT IS

Perhaps we can now make slightly clearer one of the key terms from which we started.

Judging is not in general simply accepting one of two ready-made alternatives as the right one. It cannot be done by tossing up. It is seeing reason to think and act in a particular way. It is a comprehensive function, involving our whole nature, by which we direct ourselves and find our way through a whole forest of possibilities. No science rules here; there is no given system of facts which will map our whole route for us. We are always moving into new territory.

All the same, some explicit maps and some general guidelines for explorers do exist and can be referred to. There is constant use of rationality; the area is cognitive; we can know things. We are not just guessing or gambling. Someone who takes a decision, whether about fact or value, does not usually have to leap suddenly for that purpose into a different role, in the way in which objectors to moral judgement seem to envisage. We are not, at that time, like an actor playing a stage judge who suddenly puts on wig and gown, goes into a cardboard court and becomes effectively a different person. Instead, we are committing ourselves to a decision which issues from and expresses our wider attitudes, and which has to be more or less consistent with the rest of our lives.

This consistency is, of course, never complete, because the attitudes themselves are never fully articulated. But we still need to make it as complete as possible, because the state of chaotic looseness between our various thoughts and actions is not just painful—it is destructive to our individuality, our personal identity.

Moral judgements therefore are, like other judgements, always *accountable*. We can reasonably be asked—sometimes by others and always by ourselves—to give reasons for them. We can then be expected to give those reasons from a system, however rough and incomplete, with which the rest of our lives coheres, and which is understandable both to outward and inward questioners. If these reasons are grossly unsatisfactory, we then lie under an obligation to change the judgement. We cannot simply point to a rule-book, or lay our hands on our own hearts, toss off our wigs and go away.

This obligation does not flow from any arbitrary dictation by others, but from our own nature. It is part of the condition of our existence as social, integrated, affectionate, language-using beings. The process of judging is not arbitrary; it does not stand alone; it is not something taking place beyond the borders of thought. It is continuous with the rest of life.

This view of judgment itself also does not stand alone. It is part of a whole analysis of what human individuals are, an analysis by which we shall try in this book to do justice both to their social and their individual aspects. Like all views that attempt balance, this one is not simple. But we need it, or something like it, for our lives. It should be worth our while to grasp it because we are already suffering severely from the confusions produced by the apparently simpler, more dramatic and one-sided views that have been popular lately. How the more balanced view might work will, I hope, become gradually clearer as we go on.

In this section, we have been touching on questions about the nature of knowledge which are troublesome and far-reaching. Luckily, only a small part of them overlaps with our present subject. That part, however, will occupy us again later, in chapter 17. We shall have to attend carefully to questions about what various claims to knowledge mean, and in particular about what it means to claim to know something is good or bad, right or wrong.

For instance, when John Stuart Mill made the value-judgement that I quoted earlier, saying positively that "it really is of importance not only what men do, but also what manner of men they are that do it", was he saying something that could be known or not? What sort of difference does it make whether we think of this as knowledge? These are questions about what we mean by knowledge. For the present we shall be occupied in disentangling them somewhat from others of a quite different kind. But it is perhaps worthwhile at once to ponder slightly on whether talk of knowledge about questions of value really is in some way unsuitable. For instance, is there anything wrong or misleading about what Sir John Davies says in his little poem "Man":

> I know my soul hath power to know all things,
> Yet she is blind and ignorant in all.
> I know I'm one of nature's little kings,
> Yet to the least and vilest things am thrall.

> I know my life's a pain and but a span,
> I know my sense is mocked in everything,
> And to conclude, I know myself a man,
> Which is a proud, and yet a wretched thing.

Do we really not know things of this kind? If we don't, what would knowing them be like? It is worthwhile to reflect a little about this.

NOTES

About doubt and scepticism: The liberating ideas put forward here all stem from Wittgenstein's book *On Certainty* (Oxford, Basil Blackwell, 1974) and from G.E. Moore's essay "A Defence of Common-Sense", published in his *Philosophical Papers* (London, Allen and Unwin, 1959) on which Wittgenstein was commenting. Wittgenstein's little book is not written as a continuous text but in detached remarks, requiring readers to do their own thinking. That was what Wittgenstein wanted, but he didn't always make it easy. Good background discussion can be found in *Insight and Illusion*, by P.M.S. Hacker (Oxford, Clarendon Press, 1972).

The philosophical difficulties of indiscriminate scepticism have been recently pointed out by A.C. Grayling in *The Refutation of Scepticism* (London, 1985) and by Peter Strawson in *Scepticism and Naturalism* (London, 1985). On the confusions produced by sceptical excesses in literary criticism, see *The Certainty of Literature*, by George Watson (London, Harvester Wheatsheaf, 1989). For an admirable analysis of the general ideas behind recent misdirected scepticism in ethics, see *The Sovereignty of Good*, by Iris Murdoch (London, Ark Paperbacks, Routledge, 1985).

About knowing how and knowing that, see *The Concept of Mind*, by Gilbert Ryle (London, Hutchinson, 1949), chapter 2. Ryle's essay "On Forgetting the Difference Between Right and Wrong" can be found in *Essays in Moral Philosophy*, ed. A.I. Melden (Seattle, 1958). On the relation of theoretical knowledge to the rest of life, see *From Knowledge to Wisdom*, by Nicholas Maxwell (Oxford, Blackwell, 1984), and my book *Wisdom, Information and Wonder, What Is Knowledge For?* (London, Routledge, 1989).

On the dangers of "foundationalism"—Descartes' method of piling up knowledge on a single base—see Hilary Putnam, *Reason, Truth and History* (Cambridge: Cambridge University Press, 1981).

About mistaken notions of science, see *Pluto's Republic* by Peter Medawar (Oxford University Press, 1984), and all the excellent writings of Stephen Jay Gould.

Works quoted in this chapter:

Sir John Davies, "Man", included as No. 191 in *The Oxford Book of English Verse 1250-1981*, Second Edition, ed. Sir Arthur Quiller-Couch (Oxford, Oxford University Press, 1939) p. 218.

4

Scepticism and Liberty

THE POSSIBILITY OF SCEPTICAL HUMBUG

For the moment, what has been said about knowledge here is designed only to show why the subject matters, and how important it is to distinguish these sceptical considerations about the possibility of knowledge from substantial moral considerations about the need to let other people alone and the value of freedom.

This division is slightly complicated by the fact that the sceptical considerations themselves have also a private moral motivation of their own. If we ask *why* it matters so much to find out how much we know, we at once begin to get answers centring on honesty, modesty and humility; answers that begin "It is important not to pretend to know things that we really do not know, because..."These issues too involve moral judgements that raise some quite interesting questions, for instance: is it necessarily more wicked to pretend not to know what you do know? Suppose, for instance, that a Spanish-speaking passenger on the Underground refuses to admit to having the knowledge needed to sort out an interlingual fracas? This conduct seems, on the face of it, no less dishonest and arrogant than the pretence of knowing what one does not.

This point is not very important, but it does deserve a brief mention for two reasons. First, this vague sense that honesty is always on the side of scepticism—meaning on the side of incredulity and negative answers—tends to haunt discussions about the nature of knowledge and makes it seem nobler always to *disclaim* knowing anything, however unconvincing that disclaimer may be. Second, academics have of late been narrowing the frontiers of their disciplines more and more so as to avoid being responsible for saying anything about very big questions, especially about moral questions. They have often defended this evasive habit with sceptical arguments about the impossibility of knowing the answers. This is a bad defence if one is in a position to contribute anything useful, however small and shaky, to what will in any case be a complex and many-sided investigation. It is also a dishonest defence if one then shows, in the rest of one's life, that one does in fact think the points that one might have contributed are well-established. Most of us are not in the position of the Pope; we do not need to worry about the danger of being expected to be omniscient and infallible, and we know that contributions are often needed from all sides.

LOPSIDED APPLICATIONS REVEAL FALSE UNIVERSALITY

This argument about the duty of honesty is, however, quite separate from considerations about the importance of freedom. Those are certainly the main moral considerations, that lie behind the sense of a duty not to interfere with others. People are not in general moved so much by doubt about the possibility of knowing what duty is, but by a direct, confident moral insistence on the duty of not interfering. One indication of this is the lopsided, highly selective way in which terms such as "moral judgement" are regularly used. A series of asymmetries emerges here, by which a "moral judgement" is typically conceived as:

1. a judgement about *others*, not about oneself,
2. an *unfavourable* judgement—blame or disapproval—not a favourable or neutral one,
3. an *uncharitable* judgement—that is, one not making allowance for mitigating circumstances,
4. a judgement *on an act already done*, not on one contemplated, and usually—
5. a judgement made *from a detached position*—either by a superior about subordinates, or by a spectator—not from a sympathiser or from inside the situation.

Ought we simply to straighten out this bias by becoming more thorough, more extreme? Ought we really to say, for instance, that it actually *is* just as wrong to judge the free acts of politicians as those of schizophrenics or members of oppressed minorities? Is it then just as wrong to praise a heroic rescue, or to say that there is nothing wrong with homosexual activity, as it is to blame a theft? Am I perhaps really in a position where I can no more know whether what I am myself considering doing is wrong than whether the Trobriand Islanders are wrong in their marriage customs?

Any reader who can happily answer "yes" to these and similar questions is indeed someone primarily moved by scepticism, possibly of the genuinely enquiring kind, about the nature of knowledge—a pure epistemological critic. But such people are rare. Most of us will probably answer "no", so we will want to maintain the lopsidedness just noted. If we do maintain it, it seems to follow that the quite good reasons which inspired our sweeping objections to all moral judgement were really reasons for doing something less extreme, narrower and much more useful—for objecting to certain *faulty* kinds of judgement because of their faults.

PUNISHMENT, CRUELTY AND INDIGNATION

It is no doubt worthwhile spelling out just what the faults in question are. There is a very common tendency in human societies to exploit institutions of blame and punishment by using them simply as excuses for indulging in uninhibited cruelty. In our own culture, awareness of this odious habit has been quite a late development, and it is still not at all widespread. People interviewed on these topics still do not seem to be particularly self-conscious or ashamed of displaying vindictiveness in their demand for savage and useless punishments.

The existence of this danger has long been known. Jesus drew attention to it sharply when he told those who wanted to stone the woman taken in adultery, "let him who is without sin among you cast the first stone" (St. John's Gospel, ch.8, v.7). His words in the Sermon on the Mount, "Judge not that ye be not judged", are often taken on their own as a sweeping condemnation, not just of vindictive punishment, but of the whole faculty of judgement. But this cannot be right. Jesus goes on "for with what judgement ye judge ye shall be judged" (St. Matthew's Gospel, ch.7, v.1), making the much more subtle point that while we cannot possibly avoid judging, we can see to it that we judge fairly, as we would expect others to do to us. That he did not actually mean to stop all forming and expressing of moral judgements is plain enough from the fact that he often expressed quite violent ones himself against the powerful of the earth.

In this he resembled every other serious reformer. So true is this that if we wanted to test whether a particular thinker was serious about wanting to change the world, we might simply ask, "does this writer ever make convincing accusations? Does he or she display genuine, unforced indignation against those responsible for present iniquities?" If not, we could probably safely conclude that this person was happy with things as they are. This part played by anger in our thinking is an extremely inconvenient psychological fact, granted the terrible dangers of misusing it that we have just mentioned. It is not surprising, therefore, that Jesus' words have been taken in an unrealistically extreme sense, because the exploitation of judgement by cruelty does produce lopsidedness in practice. It is blame and punishment that get an undue boost, not praise and reward, so that the whole notion of judgement is dismissed as tainted.

FURTHER DIRECTIONS

Yet it should be clear by now that this sweeping dismissal makes no sense. The kind of false universality that produces this undue sweepingness is among the most besetting temptations of all philosophical work. A good insight capable of generalisation is a precious light for our darkness, and anyone who has produced such an insight is strongly tempted to hope that its light can spread over the whole field of conceivable cases. It is almost irresistible to claim that it actually does so, but this is seldom true. Most moral insights are limited in their application. We shall meet many cases where theories have been expanded in this way beyond their useful function, and have to be carefully cut down to size.

In our present case, however, the plain preference for lopsided interpretation of the veto on moral judgement also has a consequence for the arrangement of our discussion. It shows that moral considerations are more important than those about knowledge in raising the issue at all. For this reason, it seems best in this book to deal first with these moral questions about liberty. They are so serious that, until they have been faced, it is not easy to attend properly to the more theoretical issues about knowledge and ignorance.

Out of this discussion, however, two quite good reasons for worrying about particular kinds of ignorance will indeed emerge. The first concerns what may be called *intercultural ignorance* and the obstacles it poses when we try to make moral judgements of other cultures. Alarm about this has given rise to a range of views that are roughly grouped under the name of *relativism*. These views claim that, in some sense, there are many quite separate moralities, each valid only within its own culture. The second worry is about *interpersonal ignorance*, and gives rise to various kinds of *subjectivism*—claims that people are so radically separate that each person has a quite separate morality, valid only for that person. These are two completely different and incompatible positions, though they are often served as a hotch potch together. By disentangling them, we may be in a better position to see how the kinds of scepticism that we really need can be related to a more usable, realistic view of the possibility of making moral judgements.

5

Why Must We Not Interfere?

OUTER AND INNER FREEDOM

Turning then to our outstanding moral question, we ask: how much does personal freedom matter, and why?

The idea that each individual has in some sense a *right* to be free from the interference of others is far stronger and more central to our culture than to most others, though it is of course not peculiar to it. Chinese tradition, for instance, would find our stress on that idea very surprising. The roots of this Western individualism go back at least as far as ancient Athens, but it has grown particularly fast in the last three centuries, as part of the Enlightenment.

This insistence on freedom has had two distinct stages—outer and inner. The first, which was political, was concerned with physical freedom from such gross outside interferences as being killed, maimed, imprisoned, tortured, exiled, robbed or taxed into the ground by the more powerful members of one's own society. The main reason for the creation of democratic institutions was to give citizens the power to protect themselves against these violent intrusions. More detailed questions about what things people ought to be free to do while surviving were on the whole left until later.

One question of this more detailed kind, however, already gave trouble even in the Middle Ages—namely, freedom of religion. Heresy was generally seen as a grave crime, and was severely punished. Interestingly enough, even some of the threatened heretics themselves accepted this practice, adding only that their own religion was really the orthodox one, so that it was other people who were the heretics. Thus Luther, as soon as his own doctrines were accepted in several German provinces, proposed that Anabaptists ought to be tried and burnt for heresy. This was not an eccentricity of Luther's; such views were widespread. His attitude only shows how strong and unquestioned was the idea of society as a single, homogeneous spiritual body, whose constitution could not survive the harbouring of such evils within it. Only very gradually, as the long, vile and exhausting Wars of Religion ground on in the 17th century, did the idea gain ground that variety of religious belief must somehow be tolerated. By degrees, people became used to allowing each other freedom of conscience, even on matters that might decide whether they were saved or damned.

No doubt mostly they accepted this change as a pragmatic compromise, out of sheer exhaustion and a reluctance to go on fighting, rather than because they grasped a clear set of principles that would support it. Noticing that they had not been struck by lightning for allowing heretics to survive, many people probably did conclude that God for his part must have good reasons for accepting this arrangement. But just what those reasons might be was only gradually hammered out by a succession of thoughtful Enlightenment philosophers—notably Montaigne, Locke, Rousseau, Kant, Mill, Nietzsche and Sartre. The idea that individual free choice might be, not just a regrettable necessity for public harmony, but something with a positive value in itself, was with great difficulty developed to the point where this inner freedom was presented, first as a central ideal for our culture, and finally as the supreme and even sole ideal that ought to guide it.

THE TYRANNY OF CUSTOM

John Stuart Mill's vigorous essay "On Liberty" of 1859 is something of a watershed here, a point at which the change of emphasis from outer to inner freedom is clearly proclaimed. Life and limb, said Mill, were already in his day moderately secure; citizens did not on the whole expect to be boiled in oil by robber barons. Both in Britain and in the United States, democratic political institutions were in place. But how much did these institutions actually do for individual freedom? People, said Mill, did not generally find themselves in a position in these democracies where they could do what they chose without regard to their neighbours. They were forced to live in the way that those around them expected. They were ruled by custom, by the expectations of others. As he put it, "Such phrases as 'self-government' and 'the power of the people over themselves' do not express the true state of the case. . . *The self-government spoken of is not the government of each by himself, but of each by all the rest."* (*Liberty*, p. 73). The result (Mill concluded) was simply the tyranny of the majority, the crushing of all divergent or eccentric types by the solid central mass of conventional custom and opinion. Each person was unfree internally, because the moral principles they were supposed to obey were determined by others. Even their own conscience, if it pressed them to act according to those principles, was an alien oppressor. And against this form of oppression, democratic institutions could give no protection at all—indeed they could actually make it worse.

Can this trouble be remedied? Mill concedes at once that individuals do have to accept outside control so far as their actions can injure other people. My freedom to swing my arms does have to stop short of your face. So he states his principle thus:

> The sole end for which mankind are warranted, individually or collectively, in interfering with the liberty of action of any of their number is self-protection. The only purpose for which power can be rightfully exercised over any member of a civilised community against his will, is to prevent harm to others. His own good, either physical or moral, is not a sufficient warrant.... The only part of the conduct of anyone, for which he is amenable to society, is that which concerns others. In the part which merely concerns himself, his independence is, of right, absolute. Over himself, over his own body and mind, the individual is sovereign.
>
> (*Liberty*), p.73.

This principle is familiar to us today and is the basis of many contemporary manifestos. Here is a rather more naive one from a businessman in California:

> I guess I feel like everybody on this planet is entitled to have a little bit of space, and things that detract from other people's space are kind of bad. . . one of the things that makes California such a pleasant place to live is, people by and large aren't bothered by other people's value systems as long as they don't infringe upon your own. By and large, the rule out here is that if you've

got the money, honey, you can do your thing as long as your thing doesn't destroy someone else's property, or interrupt their sleep, or bother their privacy, then that's fine. If you want to go in your house and smoke marijuana and shoot dope and get all screwed up, that's your business, but don't bring that out on the street, don't expose my children to it, just do your thing. That works out kind of neat.

(Brian Palmer, *Habits of the Heart*, pp. 6-7)

MARKING OUT THE PRIVATE SPHERE

Neat though it indeed is in some ways, this formula notoriously raises a lot of problems, some of which we shall soon have to consider. There are problems for instance about what constitutes harm, or about the possibility of having too *much* space, or about those children, or about the people who haven't got the money... However, this rough division between public and private spheres does certainly help a great deal with many practical issues. It has supplied a useful, sketchy background scheme against which we have conducted endless borderline disputes on topics such as conscientious objection, euthanasia, pornography, abortion, prostitution, blasphemy and libel, drink and drugs, variant forms of schooling, compulsion to wear seat-belts and crash helmets and all the rest. In these cases, the question "is this matter really *private*? does it affect only the person involved or does it threaten others to the point where society must intervene?" has indeed been treated as central, and often with good effect. Today, people commonly see no need to justify, or even to think about, the idea of a separate private realm that should be left undisturbed.

Mill, by contrast, had to explain and justify this idea, and it is no bad exercise for us to stand where he stood. How would we answer an actual questioner—perhaps a Chinese one—who might ask, "but how could there be any part of people's lives that does not concern those around them?" Our answer to this is not going to be a straightforward one. We are certainly not going to find some simple mistake in this questioner's point of view, some ignorance of facts or some silly slip in logic, which we need only point out in order to show why we are right on this point and those who disagree with us are wrong. What we have here is a genuine moral change, a change in values. It is a shift from emphasising the need for people to help each other to emphasising the need for them to be themselves. Because it is this sort of genuine change, we have to defend and explain it explicitly in moral terms if we want to promote it, *and this will involve making many explicit value-judgements.* That is why—as I have been suggesting—*it really is not possible to treat the change itself as putting an end to all such judging.*

WHY FREEDOM MATTERS

What, then, is the central reason why we should attend more to the claims of individuals and less to those of society? We might, of course, answer simply that, because life is safer than it used to be, less suppression of individuals is needed now to ensure survival. But if we want to argue that the suppression should actually be stopped we need more than this; we need to show that it is not just unnecessary but harmful. Mill argues this case strongly from two angles.

The first takes the point of view of suppressed individuals themselves, describing the miserable frustration of their lot and celebrating, by contrast, the splendour of the free, spontaneous activity that ought to replace it. Here, Mill repeatedly uses strong metaphors from nature. The suppressed individual is (he says) like a tree spoiled by pollarding or a bush clipped down into fancy shapes by a gardener. More sharply still, he remarks that Society's "ideal of character is to be without any marked character; to maim by compression, *like a Chinese lady's foot,* every part of human nature which stands out prominently, and tends to make the person markedly dissimilar in outline to commonplace humanity" (*Liberty*). These strong images help to build up the general value-judgement that free actions and free individuals are in themselves simply much better things—far more precious—than conditioned and automatic ones. And this judgement is now so fundamental to our moral thinking that it is not commonly attacked as too dogmatic and "judgemental".

The other prong of Mill's argument, moving in from the point of view of society itself, points out how much we all collectively stand to lose by crushing the new and original insights that our fellow citizens would contribute to social development if only we would leave them free. From this angle, therefore, there is really no conflict of interests. "In proportion to the development of his individuality, each person becomes more valuable to himself, and is therefore capable of being more valuable to others". He adds, too, that the mere variety of these distinctive individuals will itself be a public advantage, because it will be more fertile, generating far more new ideas than could be found in an intellectual monoculture. Society will always be the gainer, because "the initiation of all wise or noble things comes and must come from individuals; generally at first from one individual". On this line of thought, convergence of long-term interest should produce a happy ending satisfactory both to society and to the individual.

NOTES

The term "Enlightenment" is a rather loose one; some historians use it chiefly for movements occurring in the 17th and 18th centuries. But certain ideas, which first took shape then, are still very active in our lives, and are still developing along the lines first laid out at that time. Among these characteristic ideas, I think that Freedom is central, and I use the word "Enlightenment" to indicate a concentration on it.

To distinguish and weigh the different kinds of freedom, see *Four Essays on Liberty* by Isaiah Berlin (Oxford, Oxford University Press, 1969).

Works quoted in this chapter:

Brian Palmer, in *Habits of the Heart, Middle America Observed*, ed. Robert Bellah (London, Hutchinson, 1988), pp. 6-7

6

The Fear of Society

DRAMAS OF CONFRONTATION

Is Mill's hope that individual and public interests will converge a justified one? It is, of course, inevitably rather a distant hope. He argues well for it, yet the force and fire of his first point tend to put his second one in the shade. Here and now, this individual is interested in doing what he or she wants to do, and may not care at all whether doing it will, even in the very longest run, benefit society. Ought this individual to be asked to care? Is there anything faulty about a purely self-absorbed refusal to care? Or again, even if the individual does care, is it certain that what he or she finds good will also seem good to society? Is there any reason why the individual should take any notice of outside standards at all? Mill does not suggest that there is, and this seems to be the point at which modern Western individualism splits off from most other moralities.

To bring out this point, he uses another strong metaphor which perhaps even today is scarcely recognised as being a metaphor. He personifies Society as if it were a separate character in the drama, another person or deity standing over against all individuals and actively oppressing them. This way of talking gives a peculiar horror to the notion of conventionality, since it portrays conventional people, not as making their own mistakes, but as being somehow zombified, possessed by an alien demon that has taken over their consciences and is now directing them, using them as its mere puppets or automata. That is the sense in which they lose inner freedom.

Thus, in deploring the dreary conventionality of his age, Mill writes, "Society has now fairly got the better of individuality... From the highest class of society to the lowest, everyone lives as under the eye of a hostile and dreaded censorship" (*Liberty*). What, *everyone*? Here again, false universality is surely creeping in. Again, in discussing people distorted by bad eduction, he remarks, "Society has had absolute power over them during all the early portion of their existence... If Society lets any considerable number of its members grow up mere children, incapable of being acted on by rational consideration of distant motives, Society has itself to blame for the consequences" (*Liberty*).

This way of talking is now so familiar, and especially the idea of "blaming Society" instead of blaming any particular person is now such a cliché, that we have to make a conscious effort to see that there is anything odd about it. Yet there surely is. We seem to have lost sight here of the double capacity in which each of us must function. If everyone finds the censorship hostile and dreaded, who is imposing it? Who chooses the customs? Who, in fact, constitutes "Society"?

In these strident parts of Mill's book—only small parts, but ones which, along with other similar remarks from other writers, have had huge influence—the picture shifts from showing a community in which each of us plays both private and public roles to a drama where every one of us stands alone, detached from an uncaring universe, confronting an alien mass with which none of us is identified and for whose acts none of us is in any way responsible. To see how odd this is, we might look more carefully at Mill's remark that "the initiation of all wise or noble things comes and must come from individuals, *generally at first from one individual*". In a modest sense this does have to be true. All facts are particular facts, and when public opinion changes, somebody has to start the new ideas. People do not change direction all at once, like particles in an electric current when a switch is pressed. But does it follow that that clever somebody is solitary, that there is no co-operation, no joint work, no mutual inspiration at this point?

KEEPING COMPANY

This exaltation of solitude is not realistic. Even the most rebellious and individualistic of thinkers—even Rousseau or Nietzsche or Camus—starts from a pre-existing tradition, uses a whole mass of accepted ideas as a starting point, and also desperately wants suitable friends with whom to talk things out. None of us, not even these innovators, can start our moral business alone unless we already have a super-ego, a functioning conscience that uses a set of internalised standards originally drawn from those around us. We need this background exactly as, in order to talk, we need an existing language to speak, a language already spoken by the people we talk to. We shall learn other languages and develop other moral ideas later, but even in making these changes we shall always owe a great deal to our original base, and also to those around us who share it.

Nietzsche, who fiercely resented this dependence, vigorously abused a great range of people—notably Kant, Schopenhauer and Wagner— from whom he had learnt essential lessons, and whose thought he then went on to develop so well. But this Oedipal resentment cannot annul the dependence. Similarly, the rebellious people just mentioned often complain that they cannot get the kind of helpers they want, but they do not say that they need no helpers, nor that they would have done just as well if they had been thrown in at the beginning of history.

All this interdependence is sometimes admitted, but with agony and regret, as if it still constituted an alien invasion, a poison from which individuals cannot escape. Here we should surely look at the original conditions under which tradition is handed on. Primarily, children learn from their parents, which means that, in spite of normal ambivalence, there is a great flood of love on both sides. This love is not a trap, but a life-giving element, a context like air or water that is necessary for mental life. The child, loving the parents and others around it, really wants to absorb what it is given and therefore does so freely, actively and by its wish, not at all in the manner of an automaton or a zombie. Thus the conscience, though formed to some extent by internalisation, is not originally an alien intruder, but a genuine voluntary function of the growing person.

Of course this is not to say that the transmission goes smoothly. There is, of course, ambivalence on both sides; there is the counterweight of bitterness, anger and resentment that, in every close relation, always accompanies love. To get near to people is to collide with them. And as time goes on, this ambivalence gives force to the criticisms that the child gradually comes to make of its heritage. Ideally this should make possible just the degree of independence that it needs to form its own standards. When things are not ideal—which is usually—the dependence and resentment are in some way distorted and misplaced. Savage hostility to some aspects of the parents' tradition can then easily accompany abject submission to others. Yet this still does not mean that the conscience, along with the whole background of standards that it accepts, is an alien intrusion, nor that the outward "Society" which shares those standards is simply an enemy.

THE USES OF TRADITION

It is worthwhile to develop this theme a little, because the ideal of rootless, solitary originality has in our century been a very powerful and effective one. But like all powerful ideas it has its limits. The nature of these limits can perhaps best be seen in reference to the arts, the very place where the value of the idea has been most obvious. No human enterprise can start, as it were, suddenly in mid-air; all of them grow somewhere and have roots. This need for a context is particularly notable in the performing arts, such as music or drama. Composers and dramatists, however original, need a long and very complex tradition to start from. They must have a language to speak, an art to practise, and skilled fellow-practitioners who will effectively perform what they compose. If they were born in a culture where their arts were unknown, incomparably less scope would be open to them. Though human beings undoubtedly share some natural tastes and tendencies that point them towards the arts, the business of actually building up those arts as going concerns has been a long and weary task, a vast communal effort. That effort is what provides new entrants with their necessary working equipment. It provides not just rich and nourishing experiences and usable models, but also the trained performers, instruments, theatres, scenery, concert-halls, educated audiences and a whole mass of expectations that can make it possible for their innovations to have a meaning.

The romantic ideal of a totally fresh start, of a "modern" movement owing nothing to any predecessors—a popular idea at the beginning of the 20th century—is, if taken literally, something of a fantasy. Very good art was indeed produced at that time by people making certain limited changes. But in hindsight, the continuity of their art with its predecessors is obvious, and the effort of theorists to show that all its merits derive from its "modern" or unprecedented qualities are not convincing. Without a pre-existing framework of shared tradition, all words and notes would be indistinguishable and unmeaning noises. This is a general point about the nature of meaning. Where no patterns of expectations have been formed, nothing signifies and nothing surprises. In that situation, aspiring innovators might just as well be dumb and their hearers deaf. It is only within a coherent society and a coherent tradition of expectation that signs can mean anything at all.

WHAT IS SOCIETY?

The question then is: does this nurturing background form part of what we ought to call "Society", or not? When we think of Society in Mill's terms, as an alien ogre, such a nurturing function seems impossible. That is the mood in which revolutionaries understandably call for an entirely new start, as Omar Khayyam did:

> Ah love! could thou and I with Fate conspire
> To grasp this sorry Scheme of Things entire,
> Would we not shatter it to bits—and then
> Remould it nearer to the Heart's Desire?

Omar's metaphor represents Society as clay—or perhaps as a construction of toy bricks, needing no mortar? But as many destructive projects have now shown, Society turns out to be something organic, something much more like a forest or an ecosystem. Odious though social traditions often are, and much though they often need pruning and clearing, they are the only possible starting-point for change, and some sort of continuity in change is needed for our spiritual survival. Moreover, when bad customs are cleared, new ones have to be allowed some time to grow back again before they can support new life. It is interesting to notice how hard people in nations formed by colonisation such as Australia and the United States have at first found it to develop their own distinctive art. It had to grow. People who want to do the instant remoulding that Omar recommended tend to be disappointed, because the regrowth has to be a long and communal enterprise.

7

—

The Public Side of Morality

WHAT MORALITY IS

About the arts, this need for continuity may be fairly obvious. But we need to notice that it also holds for ideas and wider ways of living. Conceptual structures, too, are publicly shared, long-lasting things with a slow growth of their own. We can influence them—often much more than we know—but we cannot suddenly shatter them or suddenly invent new ones to our personal taste. They are much more like the forest in which we live our whole lives, or the ground on which we walk, than they are like toy houses that we can build and shatter at our whim. They therefore play a crucial part in shaping our knowledge, and they make it a much less chancy, less private, less arbitrary business than sceptics have often suggested. When we come to discuss questions about knowledge in chapter 17, this will prove important.

It is also important for morality. As we have already noticed, from one angle, morality too is undoubtedly a large-scale, public, long-term framework. The standards we appeal to in even our most startling judgements, the very words we use for praise or blame, are parts of our culture, evolved over a long time and understood by many people. Without this background, we could not speak or think coherently on such subjects at all. When each of us makes a moral judgement—for instance condemning brutal punishment or praising independence—we are using ideas and appealing to attitudes that we can expect other people to share and understand. We are not just proclaiming, suddenly and arbitrarily, an inexplicable, volcanic individual reaction. If we do do that, we know that we cannot expect other people to understand us, and that this will make it impossible for them to take seriously what we say.

Yet, on the other hand, morality does also have its private, personal aspect. Individual conscience is central to it. All of us can vary traditional judgements, even say that they are wrong. We can criticise and refine existing standards, and in this way we can gradually change them. There is, however, a difficulty in doing this, a difficulty connected with the other, more public aspect of moral business. The language for the change often is not ready-made for us.

There is, in fact, a constant friction—here and in every other department of language—between existing concepts and the half-formed thought we are trying to develop. That is why new words and phrases are coined, and why old words change their meaning. For instance, when Christianity wanted to introduce powerful ideas of charity and mercy into cultures uncritical of callousness and used to bloody-minded retribution, it needed to change the language of praise and blame radically—a task that is not yet completed. Again, in the development of the modern Enlightenment virtues of tolerance and humaneness, new words had to be coined, new analogies pressed before usable concepts could eventually be formed.

THE SOCIAL ROLE OF PRIVATE CONSCIENCE

Moralists and poets, philosophers and historians and sages of all kinds as well as ordinary people, have to work hard and long to restate things in a way that makes these changes intelligible. And those who have struggled, as Mill and Kant did, to liberate the individual conscience from social pressures have been aiming, not just to make individuals free and happy, but also to make them capable of undertaking this work of moral creativity—of generating new practical concepts. They wanted the kind of inner freedom in which the conscience can be much more than a mere conformist super-ego—more than an internalised parent-figure policing traditional standards. They wanted it to find strength to act critically and rationally so that it could create new ones.

When this is actually done, however, the new ideas in their turn become public property. They do not remain as private playthings of those who first conceived them. Morality—like art—thus continues to have both a public and a private aspect, and this double function seems to be unavoidable. But people disputing about the boundaries of liberty have made various efforts to avoid it by splitting off one element or the other. Mill for his part, attached the word "morality" firmly to the public sphere, contrasting it with liberty. In his language, "whenever there is a definite damage, or a definite risk of damage, either to an individual or to the public, the case is *taken out of the province of liberty, and placed in that of morality or law"* (*Liberty*, p. 138). In this usage morality too, like Society, stands out as an alien force over against the individual and is easily seen as an enemy.

The other obvious way of speaking is to say that the public sphere is ✓ that of law and custom, while morality is a private matter, ruled only by the individual conscience. This seems a more natural use in that it allows more weight and seriousness to the workings of that conscience. But since it allows it no scope to affect the outside world, nor even to judge it, the function of such a purely private conscience turns out to be disturbingly limited. For instance, a conscientious objector to military service might, on this view, claim exemption for himself on moral grounds, and might somehow convince a tribunal that he should have it. But this same objector could not properly have or express an opinion about the arguments by which others might justify their decision to fight, nor about whether the claims of any other objectors than himself were justified. Nor is it easy to see how a tribunal that was called on to assess these various claims could possibly attempt to do so. on an individual basis – case by case!

FREEDOM AND EDUCATION

Altogether, there are great difficulties about the idea of morality as purely a private, individual function, difficulties that arise because it is then conceived as working without the common, shared, historically developed background that, in actual life, we always use to make it understandable. I have suggested that the need for this kind of background is familiar, and should not strike us as damaging to freedom, because we appeal to it also in the case of the arts.

Obviously, too, background is essential for education. In the last two centuries, Western educationists have stressed the need for freedom, for allowing a child to generate ideas spontaneously rather than being handed them ready-made. This has obviously been of immense value, yet it cannot be the whole story. Children often react disappointingly to a careful restriction of input. They want to hear stories and indeed to be given directions. They like to let their imaginations play spontaneously, but they do not want to play all the time. They are also curious to know more facts and to gain usable ideas to help them handle those facts. And they know that they need to absorb the general map of existing ideas—including moral ideas—on how to live before they will be in any position to help in the development of new ones. They must take what society can give them and learn how it works before they can hope to change it.

But of course, much of it doesn't work!

ORIGINALITY AND CONTINUITY

This does not of course mean that the hostility to tradition, and to the weight of "Society" in general, has been a mere mistake. As so often happens, a genuine point has been exaggerated. Of course the reformers were right to think that education was not just a matter of learning received views by heart. But it cannot follow that education need not pass on tradition at all. Similarly, the art critics who made a fetish of the idea of "the modern" were often right to praise certain particular new departures, but wrong in their knee-jerk response of dismissing everything old just because it was old.

This more complicated situation is being recognised today in the current reaction against this particular cult of the modern, tending to replace it by a cult of our traditional heritage. Of course this reaction too can become absurd, but it surely has some sense in it. To insist, habitually and on principle, on favouring only art or thought that is modern would be a policy of planned obsolescence. It would require us, after a certain interval, ruthlessly to junk Picasso, Gropius and Stravinsky, Einstein and Wittgenstein and Martin Buber, in order to make room for their successors—that is, for the latest fashion, whatever that fashion might happen to be. (The word "modern", after all, just means fashionable.)

Perhaps it is surprising that champions of "the modern" have not usually done this. Instead, with a rather touching loyalty, they have gone on treating early 20th-century figures as modern by definition. That is why the still more unhelpful word "post-modern" has now had to be coined and is being used for a jumble of different ideas which have nothing in common except that they happen to have followed the early 20th-century set, thus acquiring, at present, the prestige that attaches to the latest fashion. In another decade they will, of course, have to be renamed.

In the last three chapters we have been discussing the idea of non-interference as a central human duty and the notion of inner freedom as detachment from society which has been developed in response to it. This has brought us to consider what kind and degree of detachment individuals can actually endure, and what kind of background continuity—both in contemporary society and in tradition—they may actually need for any serious kind of survival.

Many elements in this problem are timeless and unchanging, parts of the natural condition of the human race. But as we have seen, others are strictly contemporary matters, changes arising out of the incredibly rapid, large-scale changes that mark our time. It is important to distinguish between these two kinds of difficulty. As we have noticed, the temptation of theorists is always toward a false, premature universality, a tendency to exalt temporary, local responses into cosmic truths, and to freeze the methods of thought to fit them. In our present epoch of rapid change, this is particularly unfortunate and wasteful. It will therefore be worth our while to attend to some factors in our present-day version of individualism which have been treated as timeless and universal, but which seem to have quite particular roots in the conditions of our times.

8

Individuals in the Modern Melting-Pot

THE PROGRESSIVE ESCALATOR

For well over a century now, people in the West have felt much confidence in the idea that they could get guidance simply from the direction in which they were already travelling. They have been strongly gripped by the thought that the rapid changes taking place in their civilisation were carrying them along a straight, upward path or escalator of progress (or advance, or evolution) towards an ideal condition.

This meant that any doubts arising about the next step could in principle always be resolved by deciding to press on, to make *more* changes of the kind that they had just been making. Thus, if the population, or the speed of travel, or the size of towns had recently been multiplied by five, the progressive next step should always be to repeat that process—moving as far and as fast as possible in a fixed direction—away from the *status quo*. The odious phrase "dragging people kicking and screaming into the 20th century" has been freely used by people who felt themselves to be safely placed in this way on an upward escalator, and their attitude has apparently been too widely accepted for such phrases to attract the criticism that their brutality might normally have been expected to earn.

Of course that simple-minded optimism has never been universal. All the same, this kind of feeling has been and still is a real force in our lives. Even though the last few decades have given us so many bitter warnings about the effects of a naïve linear approach, it still pervades much of our thought and terminology. For instance, the language of art-criticism is still dominated by the image of the avant-garde, which means a body marching ahead of the rest of the army. But along what road? Unless there is some definite journey to be made, some particular enemy to be conquered, the mere fact of moving away fast has no point. (In the 19th century, of course, the enemy ahead was the art establishment. But today much of the art establishment identifies itself officially with the avant-garde, which makes the position itself quite remarkably confusing.) Similarly, when we want to call for some human or liberating policy, we often do it merely by calling it progressive, or by using such phrases as "it's the next step", or "it has to come", and by calling the present inhumane conditions "outdated" or "Victorian" or "mediaeval". Moreover, when something odious is introduced, the objection to it tends to be stated merely in terms of its being old-fashioned.

The habit of talking as if the mere fact that something is out of fashion is a sufficient objection to it, instead of taking the trouble to think out what is really wrong, is an unsatisfactory habit in at least four ways. (1) It is a most unhistorical thing, since these conditions are often quite recent aberrations. (2) By no means everything that is out of fashion actually is wrong anyway; we may be simply being misled. There is an extraordinary notion prevalent among intellectuals in our times that certain things have "become impossible" or that some art form "is dead", when all that has happened is that the fashion has changed slightly. (3) It saves us the trouble of thinking what actually *is* wrong with the existing conditions, which would force us to aim more accurately to get rid of that wrong thing. And (4) it is bad because it fosters in us the notion that we do have a fixed upward escalator carrying us to a predetermined goal, a salvation on earth that will surely be provided independent of our own efforts.

To repeat: this belief has of course not been as simple-minded as I am suggesting, and of course it has been only one thread in our thinking, constantly contending against all sorts of other tendencies. All the same, it has been a powerful and distinctive vision. It has also been a very strange one in that it has been used to recommend an amazing range of quite different things as "modern" or "progressive", since many different paths actually have been travelled, and none has been anything like as straight as the image suggests.

This reliance on a shifting ideal of modernness is now producing such odd effects that it seems worth while to ask just *why* that particular kind of exaggeration—that somewhat frantic rejection of traditional social background and flight to an unknown future—should have become so powerful at this time in the first place. Why have people during the last two centuries developed such a strong hope that change must always be for the better, such a horror of their social roots?

PROGRESS AND SCIENCE

It is sometimes thought that this glorification of linear change has its source in science, that the picture of upward progress is justified by the Darwinian theory of evolution. But this is a mistake. Interestingly enough, this escalator picture does not actually belong to biology at all. Darwin's theory of evolution simply explains the way in which organisms adapt to changing circumstances, and says nothing about any fixed upward direction. Darwin himself saw no reason to suppose that there was any such fixed upward direction, and only used the word evolution once in his writings. His scientific heirs today, though they use the word, still do not attach that upward meaning to it. The notion of upward linear movement, along with this use of the word evolution, come from Lamarck, Herbert Spencer and other sages quite remote from modern science.

This escalator-faith does not rest on scientific evidence: its roots are spiritual or psychological. We may choose to believe in inevitable progress because it makes our efforts easier, or from religious belief, but we do so as a matter of faith, not of science. One obvious source of this faith is, of course, the displaced religious feeling that surges around looking for adequate objects among people exiled in one way or another from the established religions. But this does not seem to me a sufficient explanation for the remarkable shift we have made from thinking—as people traditionally have thought—that things used to be better in the past, to thinking that they will certainly be better in the future, and from the declared policy of trying to preserve what we have to the declared policy of trying to change it completely.

LONELY CROWDS

This change surely has social roots, sources lying in the changed relation between individuals and their societies. It testifies, I think, mainly to the pressure of anonymous crowds—the sheer increase in numbers and in mobility in modern society. Up until a century and a half ago, people in our culture, as in most others, spent nearly all their lives in a fixed and fairly narrow circle. Though that circle was in a way constricted, they had time to get used to their world and to understand how it worked. They knew personally most of those around them and were in turn well-known to them. Though their power might have been very limited, they had an equally limited circle to exercise it in. Within that circle, they were able to hope to make their personal mark and to be noticed and remembered.

When, however, the Industrial Revolution spilled these people out into the swelling towns, they were at once surrounded by crowds of strangers. The trouble was not only that—as Marx pointed out—they were alienated from their work, they were also alienated from the workings of the life around them. Alienation is the sense of *not belonging*, and it seems to be central to the feeling Mill noted of losing one's inner freedom. The fear is not just of being controlled, but of being controlled by something outside ourselves, something incomprehensible, something with which we do not and cannot identify at any level. In order to conform with the customs of these strangers one will need to set one's will in strange meaningless patterns, to obey, not just outside laws, but a conscience which is not really one's own.

It is important too that, at this same time, the actual workings of society were moving onto a larger and larger scale, and were also constantly changing, so that it became increasingly hard for anybody to understand them. The alarm which all this produced is not just the plain, crude sense of outside oppression, which of course had been present before the Industrial Revolution as much as after. In fact the people who expressed their alienation were often ones who were not poor, not oppressed in that outer sense at all. Thus A.E. Housman writes:

The laws of God, the laws of man,
He may keep that will and can;
Not I: let God and man decree
Laws for themselves and not for me...
And how am I to face the odds
Of man's bedevilment and God's?
I, a stranger and afraid
In a world I never made.
They will be master, right or wrong;
Though both are foolish, both are strong.

And since, my soul, we cannot fly
To Saturn or to Mercury,
Keep we must, if keep we can.
These foreign laws of God and man.

This is something different from the rebellious writing of the earlier Romantic poets, savage and intense though that had often been. Housman's bitterness, unlike Shelley's or Blake's, is fatalistic. He makes no call for action. Writing at the end of the 19th century, he saw no way in which he could identify with, and so influence, the social mass that scared him. He just disowned it. And this happened although on the face of things he was by no means a helpless or powerless person. He was indeed in most ways a quite conventional and prosperous member of the professional classes, divided from "Society" only by his homosexuality and by failing his Oxford final exams. Yet he expresses here as complete a detachment from his context as if he had been suddenly dropped from Mars.

NEW SOCIETY, NEW INDIVIDUAL

I am suggesting that the mere size of modern societies, along with the mobility that constantly shakes people about in them, has changed our perceptions of what "Society" is, making it much harder for us to keep any sense of belonging. In this crowded, confusing scene, the drama that simply sets each individual over against the whole of "Society" has much more force than it would in a smaller group. This different notion of "Society" has brought with it a different notion of what it actually means to be an individual. To exploit metaphor: where people once felt more or less like branches or leaves or fruits on a tree, they now often feel more like stones in a concrete-mixer.

Of course all such images convey only aspects of the truth, but it is especially important now for us to resist this concrete-mixer model, because it is being presented to us with special force. And it cannot possibly be right. *Society, however confused it may be, still does incorporate all of us,* and our individual actions still are the force that directs it. Housman's rejection of responsibility is itself paradoxical, for his fatalism did in fact, through his poetry, have quite a marked influence on current thought and feeling. The claim to stand outside society can be as misleading a piece of humbug as the claim to be totally at one with it.

GENERATION TROUBLE

Besides the mere size and mobility of society, however, difficulties have also sprung from the *pace* at which things have altered. In times of rapid change, gaps and conflicts between different generations become wider. The natural, universal sources of misunderstanding between parents and children are sharpened in conditions where the parents' attitudes actually are getting out of date. Adolescents who need to shape new strategies for a shifting world feel more than usually exasperated by parental obstruction, and generate new forms of rhetoric so as to protest against the existing social mass that resists them. This too makes the simple drama of defying society as a whole look appropriate. "Society" becomes a parent-figure. Young people who don't yet feel themselves to be incorporated into this society can very easily believe that they form no part of it.

From the 18th century onwards, novels, poems and plays have often centred on these efforts by young people to revolt against the authority of their elders. At first the obstructions were often purely personal and the happy ending was usually marriage, bringing a successful reintegration into society. Tragic non-conformers, however, such as Werther and Childe Harold, gradually became more prevalent in fiction during the Romantic Revival, and began to penetrate the novel, expressing a much more radical rejection. Samuel Butler's novel of 1903 *The Way of All Flesh*, which leaves its hero in a situation of fatalistic withdrawal quite close to Housman's, opened up a nihilistic approach that was strongly exploited by the spate of novels describing soldiers' experiences of horror and disillusion during the First World War.

This war seems indeed to have been the occasion that institutionalised the generation gap. It then became normal to expect that the young would be disaffected, denouncing society, not just as immoral, but as hopelessly alien. It also became something of a convention that the central characters of novels could be expected to be disaffected, isolated and detached from the life around them. These were at first young people, but later the tradition spread to characters of any age. (Again, the earlier generation of protesters had now grown old.) The loneliness of old age found expression in Samuel Beckett's startling innovation of one-person plays. There was a tendency for people of all ages to see themselves as occupying the isolated situation that typically belongs only to adolescents who do not yet see how they can find any place in the society around them.

THE AMERICAN FACTOR

In all this, developments in the USA were very important. The original generation-conflict was specially harsh among immigrants to new countries like the United States. Great masses of people were tossed together in a way that inevitably cut each of them off from the social context by which they were accustomed to make sense of life. Emigrating parents often tried to cushion this effect by bringing parts of that context with them, but their children, knowing that they had to adjust to something different, tended to reject what had been so carefully preserved. People who were stirred in this melting-pot were strongly driven to narrow their social horizons, and again, it was not only the poor who felt this pressure. Prosperous Americans, too, were driven into the various kinds of individualism that Alexis de Tocqueville noted when he visited the United States in 1830. *Individualism* was then a new word, and de Tocqueville explains what he means by it, namely:

a calm and considered feeling which disposes each citizen to isolate himself from the mass of his fellows and withdraw into the circle of family and friends; with this little society formed to his taste, he gladly leaves the greater society to look after itself... Such folk [feel that they] owe no man anything and hardly expect anything from anybody. They form the habit of thinking of themselves in isolation and imagine that their whole destiny is in their hands... Each man is forever thrown back on himself alone, and there is danger that he may be shut up in the solitude of his own heart.

(*Democracy in America*, 1988, pp.506-8)

THE PRICE OF FREEDOM

Though this spirit found its fullest growth in America, it is not something that we on this side of the Atlantic can afford to shrug off. The central ideas that made it possible were ones drawn from the European Enlightenment, and moreover the way of life that has grown out of these ideas is now of immense influence world-wide. Today, almost everywhere, the

United States is accepted as the "modern" nation *par excellence*, one some-how standing ahead of the rest on the straight path that all may have to tread, whether they want to or not. But many people everywhere also hold that we ought to want to. In spite of some recent batterings, the American way of life has been long and widely viewed as the pattern of all that is praised and valued in the modern age, as embodying the distinctively modern ideal.

No nation, and no moral vision, can for long sustain this sort of inflated position. The complex of ideals that were combined to form this idealised notion of the modern is now beginning to break up. It has to, because a good deal of its work has been done, and because many of those most closely involved with it are growing uncomfortably aware that it has contained some very unsatisfactory elements. (To spectators at a distance, notably in the Third World, it still tends to look more impressive.) At this point, it becomes essential to sort out the better from the worse elements that are combined in this notion of what is "modern" or "enlightened", what constitutes "progress".

A central factor is undoubtedly this individualism that we have been considering, this special emphasis on freedom—this attempt to detach each person from any traditional and hierarchical bonds that might frustrate a completely independent, autonomous development. It is a spirit that has served to bring about countless reforms that we all value—the forging of representative democracy, the abolition of slavery and capital punishment, the partial emancipation of women, universal education, the restriction of working hours and all the rest of it. Inadequate though these things are, if they were taken away we should soon know how much we value them, and we still do rely on the individualistic spirit to help us in carrying this work further. Its business is by no means finished; there is plenty of hierarchical oppression still around. Yet the costs, the limits of this approach are already becoming pressing.

We could sum these costs up crudely by saying: first, that the sources of human unhappiness are shifting to centre more and more on social isolation. Oppressed people today are increasingly likely to suffer, not just from old-fashioned outside oppression, but from loneliness as well. They may have space all right, because nobody comes near them, but that space may not prove to be all that they want.

FORGETTING THE BIOSPHERE

Second, as we now know, here is another very serious range of costs that are not borne by human beings at all, but by non-human nature. In exalting human individuals as the sole bearers of value, individualism has unthinkingly licensed the uncontrolled exploitation of all other life-forms. Brutality on an unparalleled scale towards other animals in mechanised farming, extraordinary destructiveness towards plant life have been freely practised by a civilisation that has supposed itself, at a conscious level, to be exceptionally sensitive and humane, and has indeed often made great efforts to be so.

In one way, this negligence has sprung from ignorance, caused by that same confusing vastness of modern society just mentioned. Most Western people simply did not know about the destruction of the tropical forests until it began to appear recently on their television screens, and those few who did know about it mostly did not grasp what it meant. Similarly, most people have had no idea of what went on in factory "farms" until these activities lately too began to force themselves on public attention because their effects were poisoning human beings. But this ignorance is not just normal ignorance. It has also been a wish not to know. It has been constantly deepened and protected by an ideology which ruled that these things could not matter.

Until very lately, ecological and human campaigners were again and again warded off from reaching the public consciousness by the widely-held attitude that nothing non-human could seriously concern human beings. This attitude has involved in the first place a factual belief that human prosperity could continue indefinitely whatever people did to the rest of the biosphere—a belief which is now crumbling fast under repeated hammer-blows from the contrary evidence. But it involved, too, a moral judgement that non-human beings were not so important—that humans owed them no duty. And as so often happens, the reasoning here has run mainly from values to facts. If the value-judgement that condemned non-human nature as worthless had not been present, the very eccentric factual belief that we could safely neglect it would scarcely have been so widely accepted.

NOTES

About Individualism: To avoid getting caught (as so many people have been) inside the incurably solitary self proposed by Descartes, see *I and Thou* by Martin Buber (Edinburgh, R. & H. Clark, 1945). Also Bishop Butler's *Sermons*, especially a series of splendid footnotes answering Hobbes. Butler was a man of remarkable commonsense, who spotted at once the element of nonsense in the Social Contract Myth, and therefore spelt out plainly the limitations that were necessary to its use. Since that myth has been enormously powerful in the last three centuries, this work has never had the attention that it should have had. Now that contractual, competitive individualism is beginning to give way beneath us, some rethinking of Butler's kind is becoming absolutely necessary.

Works quoted in this chapter:

A.E. Housman, *Last Poems* XII (1922). More recently published in *The New Oxford Book of Victorian Verse*, ed. Christopher Ricks (Oxford, Oxford University Press, 1987) pp. 613-4

Alexis de Tocqueville, *Democracy in America* (trans. Lawrence, New York, Harper and Row, 1988) p. 508

9

Individualism, Solitude and Privacy

THE EXALTATION OF INDEPENDENCE

In our present discussion we are chiefly concerned to look, not at nature, but at the individualistic view of relations between human beings. And here there does seem to be something strange in the idealisation of solitude. Human beings are not limpets or even crocodiles, they are highly social creatures. Except for a few natural hermits, they have to interact fairly constantly if they are to have any sort of a satisfying life. And these interactions are only possible where there is some measure of agreement on basic patterns, patterns that are provided partly by universal natural tendencies and partly by each particular culture.

These patterns are needed to make possible deeply satisfying experiences such as those provided by the arts, crafts, sports and sciences, and also complex personal relations. But inevitably they do often frustrate individual wishes. For instance, whatever sexual mores are adopted, people are always liable to want something that others do not wish to grant them, and so to be frustrated. At present, novel after novel points out the unreality of hoping, as people apparently did at mid-century, to provide equally for everybody's sexual tastes simply by ruling that anything goes.

This difficulty brings out well the point mentioned earlier that we cannot live on a tolerance which proceeds merely from detached indifference, an undiscriminating tolerance such as might be accorded to alien beings. Most forms of sex need positive co-operation, which is only possible where the parties share similar ideas on what they want to do—on the importance it is to have in their lives—and on how long it is expected to go on. The attempt to accept everything equally has notoriously produced a situation where leanings towards constancy or chastity can be hard to accommodate, and are indeed liable to be frowned on as perversions. Composers of early 20th-century Utopias, such as Shaw and H.G. Wells, tended to deal with this difficulty by claiming that people in ideal future conditions would be so emancipated that they would have learnt not to attach any real importance to sexual relations, or indeed to personal relations generally. They would take these things in their stride; they would be mature enough not to mind who they slept with or indeed who they talked with. However, things haven't worked out that way.

Of course this difficulty is not confined to sex but affects all kinds of social intercourse. We live our lives by all sorts of unspoken but shared assumptions about such things as whether friendships are expected to be lasting—whether and when they will naturally give way to family or business concerns—what sort of confidentiality they involve and a hundred other points on which clashes and misunderstandings can be disastrous. This becomes clear at once on visits abroad, and of course clearer still in cross-cultural marriages.

INDIVIDUALISTIC EXTREMES

At a deeper level, too, these expectations mould individuals by entering into the formation of their thoughts and feelings throughout their lives. Only to a very limited extent can any of us be called "autonomous" or self-legislating. A child growing up with no background culture at all would have a very thin and shaky life, not an enriched one. Giving children a normal cultural heritage is not an interference, but an act of normal provision for human life. Indeed, if every kind of input that affected us were to count as interference, the whole idea of interference as something objectionable would lose its meaning.

This notion of complete solitary independence, going far beyond what de Tocqueville described as existing in his day, may sound bizarre, but it needs to be thought about because it does have some influence today. It is certainly the terminus towards which individualism points us. People today often feel a certain guilt because they do not really want it, because they are not independent enough—a surprising piece of morality which has even penetrated feminist writing. The mutual dependence in which we all quite rightly live with those around us is often viewed with a strange kind of puritanical disapproval, as some kind of illicit indulgence. It is one aim of this book to draw attention to the oddness of this moral view. Indeed we do sometimes need the courage and honesty to act alone, without the support of others. But there is surely no reason to suggest that it ought to be our ambition to *live* alone. The ideal of relying on no one but oneself seems a strangely thin and negative one. It would be better, one might suppose, to aim at being someone on whom others could rely, when necessary.

Extreme individualism, which altogether rejects "society", is then a particular kind of moral view—again, almost certainly a piece of false universality. (We will look at it more fully in considering subjectivism in chapters 13 to 15.) It is not compulsory, any more than extreme corporatism, which might lead us to submerge ourselves entirely in society, is compulsory. To accept either extreme would be to make a very strong, distinctive moral judgement, and the very possibility of moral judgements is (we may remember) just what we are trying to investigate. But we do need to take serious notice of individualism because it is very powerful in the modern world. In particular, it has played a great part in generating the problems we are now considering, about the possibility of judgement and the general relevance of thought to life. But we certainly should not regard it as our doom, as something that we have to accept and carry further simply because we happen to have been born in the 20th century.

MODERATE INDIVIDUALISM; PUBLIC AND PRIVATE SPHERES

What about the more moderate notion that Mill expressed, of simply preventing interference—noseyparkering of an ordinary, recognised kind—by insulating people's moral views within a private sphere? Can we manage to co-exist in society at a practical level while letting everybody pursue their own private morality? Can we arrange a compromise, regulating public life purely by convenience—by agreeing on certain simple rules that are not supposed to have any moral force, like the rule of the road—while leaving each person to regulate his or her own private life according to his or her chosen morality? Is this a way by which the objectionable kind of moral judgement—the adverse kind that people form about each other—could be altogether eliminated?

This is quite an influential contemporary view, and up to a point indeed it has been implemented. The law does not now compel us all to go to the national church, or to wear clothes suited to our station. It does not forbid us to play football or to celebrate Christmas or to gamble or drink wine or to go to the theatre or to commit adultery—all of which things have in various times and places been offences punishable by law. Most of us would probably approve of this restriction of the legal sphere, sometimes because we do not believe these things to be wrong, sometimes because we think that, even if they are wrong, the law is not the best way to control them—any more than it is the best way to stop us telling lies or losing our tempers.

But the present suggestion goes far beyond this. It exempts the private sphere, not just from the law, but also from morality—that is, from the morality of everyone except the individuals involved. In accordance with the manifesto from which we originally set out, it forbids all moral judgement about the private affairs of others. (Their public affairs are handled by law and custom, directed by principles of convenience.) What, however, determines the boundary of this private sphere? What makes certain things private?

FRONT-DOOR PRIVACY

Brian Palmer, the Californian businessman quoted earlier, takes a quite common line here, relying largely on front-doors. "Don't bring that out on the street" he says, referring to drug-taking of a kind to which he objects. What, however, if those inside the house are bullying their children or tormenting their grandmothers? More kinds of acts can go on behind closed doors than he suggests, and strange things can emerge when doors are finally opened. Of course doors constitute a barrier. It can be hard both for the law and for the neighbours to discover or remedy what goes on behind them. But it can hardly follow from this that no moral question arises about these things for anyone outside. It cannot be true that what happens inside villa Number 12 is a topic on which no one who lives anywhere else is entitled to have any moral opinion.

Palmer explains that Californians "aren't bothered by other people's value-systems". Here he is concentrating—as people so often do when they talk about values or morals—on a special, quite narrow range of activities, centrally sexual ones, which many people now genuinely think not to be wrong provided that they are not dangerous. This view has not just been invented in California. A century back, Mrs Patrick Campbell reasonably disclaimed interest in what people did sexually provided that they didn't do it in the street and frighten the horses. *But the judgement that these things are not wrong, and the judgement that child-abuse is wrong, are both moral judgements.* Unless people in general are agreed on these judgements, the idea of a private sphere will not work.

This becomes clear if we notice how our view of the situation would change if it involved a group of neighbours who were all abusing their children, and who had agreed, from motives of prudence, not to interfere with each other in doing so. For a long time indeed, our law did protect the beating of children by their parents, and also of wives by their husbands—not only behind closed doors, but anywhere. These were supposed to be purely private matters. This ruling, however, was not supposed to be just a prudential bargain; it was defended as an institution that those who formed and administered the law actually approved of. That too was a distinct moral view, for which they gave reasons. They exalted the rights of male householders to rule freely and without impediment over their families as more important than the rights of other family-members not to be beaten. This (rather obviously interested) moral judgement was long and stoutly defended on the grounds of privacy; since it was held that what took place within the family was no moral business of anybody outside. Ultimately, however, this defence collapsed because moral judgement on the matter changed in society as a whole. When this happened, the abuse of wives and children moved out of the private sphere and became recognised as a matter of public concern.

This example of domestic abuse may serve to show that the idea of morality lies deeper than that of a private sphere marked off by families or by front-doors, and cannot be dissolved into that idea. We do not each have a separate morality, and a separate private province in which to deploy it, as we might each have differently-coloured fish and put them into our own personalised fish-tanks. Instead, there is a shared morality, one inside which we all live and to whose developments we all contribute.

Like our atmosphere, this morality is held in common even though each
of us uses and perceives it rather differently. Front doors are indeed
barriers to burglars, to policing and to unmannerly intrusion, but not to
moral judgement. People who live in separate houses are still unavoidably
members of one another.

NOTES

George Bernard Shaw's Utopia, or dream of a perfect future, is expressed
in his play *Back to Methuselah*. Wells wrote a number of such prophecies, of
which the best-known are *A Modern Utopia* and *Men Like Gods*. Since the time
of Shaw and Wells, Utopias have (rather interestingly) gone out of fashion,
and been largely replaced by "dystopias" or fantasies of a world far worse
than the one we have now.

10

Morality and Harm

ONE-PERSON PRIVACY; THE CRITERION OF HARM TO OTHERS

Is it possible to express the notion of a private moral sphere in a more workable way than that offered by the front-door version, by concentrating it simply on the idea of individual harm and advantage? This is the path that Mill chose, insisting that each individual may only be controlled by society in order to stop him or her doing harm to others. He stated this in rather surprising language drawn from political theory. "In the part [of his conduct] which merely concerns himself, his independence is, of right, *absolute*. Over himself, over his own body and mind, the individual is *sovereign*" (*Liberty*, p.73).

The language is surprising because it might seem natural for somebody taking Mill's position to get rid of concepts like absoluteness and sovereignty altogether. And perhaps indeed that would have been the wiser method. At a simple level Mill's principle has of course been of immense use in restraining all sorts of petty and pointless tyranny. If, however, it is strictly pressed over the whole range of cases—if we make a serious attempt to treat independence as absolute—the principle proves unworkable unless a whole mass of extra moral judgements are put in to supply a suitable background. Clearly, it raises two main sets of difficulties.

1. HARMING ONESELF

In the first place, it is not even clear that harm to oneself does always fall outside morality. Suppose that somebody starts chopping off the joints of his fingers, one by one, in the middle of Trafalgar Square. When people object, this person says, "Oh sorry, I didn't know it would upset you. Of course I understand that being upset is harmful, and that I mustn't do harm to anybody except myself. So I'll go home and do it there". Will this retreat to front-door privacy satisfy the critics? Serious self-destructiveness in others is not just something that people dislike, a matter of taste, like a raucous voice or a rough manner. It is also something they disapprove of. Most people, if they are made aware of an impending suicide or self-mutilation, will think it right to make considerable efforts to prevent it, and will not think that doing so is illicit interference. And if the person doing these things is rational enough to discuss them, they will have no hesitation in telling him or her that the acts are wrong.

This does not, of course, mean that suicide can never be justified. In particular cases, strong arguments can be produced to show that it is actually rational for a person to choose to die. But these arguments must be ones that can be shown to be strong. They cannot just be bypassed by saying that suicide is a private affair. Some people, too, hold that such arguments can never be strong enough to justify self-destruction, which is why euthanasia—painless death by one's own desire and consent—remains a controversial issue.

When, then, we say an action must be allowed because it is private, we do not just mean that it affects nobody but the person who does it. We mean more than that. We mean that we have decided that this act is in general *not wrong*, and this is a moral judgement. If, therefore, we are to institutionalise this tolerance as a widespread system, we need to have general moral agreement on what is wrong and what is not.

2. HARMING OTHER PEOPLE

What about other people? If we say that doing needless harm to them is always wrong, we are already committed to making at least this one large moral judgement in common. (There could certainly be eccentric, purely egoistic moral systems which would deny this judgement, and there are many partial and hierarchical ones which do claim to justify harming certain kinds of people.) Then too, in order to draw our borderline, we need agreement as well on what constitutes harm, and what are the kinds of necessity that could justify it. Is it harmful, for a start, to employ people in ways that might be thought objectionable? Economic pressures can be very strong. Is it justifiable to pay somebody to act as a prostitute, a drug-pusher, a slaughterhouse-operative or a scientist in a factory making chemical weapons? And again, what about particular kinds of persuasion, influence and propaganda? Can some forms of these things be called undoubtedly harmful and corrupting, or is that an arbitrary matter, to be settled by each person's individual taste?

These are areas where background moral judgements about the general nature of the activity make all the difference, and therefore ones where controversy is hottest, as may easily be seen by reading the letters in any newspaper. Thus, a correspondent writing to the *Guardian* on August 4, 1989, about sectarian schools declared sweepingly, "Instilling beliefs in children is a form of child-abuse... What poses as freedom of belief in this country encompasses the freedom to brainwash your child."

This writer, like so many others, clearly had in mind only one particular set of beliefs. But there are many kinds, and every belief has its opposite. And on any question that a child thinks about and asks about at all, the refusal of parents to instil one belief will often strike the child simply as an endorsement of the opposite one. You can easily instil atheism, or contempt for religion, or for particular views on what religion should be like, and you can do this simply by the way in which you refuse to answer questions about them. Or you can equally instil the idea that the whole topic is distressingly embarrassing, even obscene, and that decent people do not talk about it. But what nobody can do is to suppress a child's natural curiosity to know what its elders' views are on important subjects, nor its tendency to adopt these views provisionally until it finds some reason to reject them.

"Brainwashing" is something quite different—a special set of techniques for deliberately destroying a person's existing, naturally-formed belief-system in order to replace it with one chosen by the brainwasher. But the ordinary, natural way in which people form their own belief-systems is by taking all kinds of material from those around them, and gradually making their own selection from it. There is no available option of isolating children from influence altogether.

CHILDREN AND OTHERS

These questions about indoctrination come up with special force about children, and it is interesting to notice how confidently Brian Palmer reacts to the shooting of dope in their presence. "Don't expose my children to it," he says firmly. But why not? There are contemporary sages, such as Timothy Leary and even Aldous Huxley, whose value-systems indicate that dope-shooting is no harm at all, but a benefit. Children, after all, are separate individuals, and a strict observance of one-person individualism ought surely to let them make their own separate judgements.

The case of children has always been a puzzle for individualistic thinking. The earliest Enlightenment sages did not pay much attention to it, because they were bent above all on getting their representatives into positions of political power. For those purposes they used a very simple Social Contract model in which only male householders counted as people. They relied confidently on slogans like "the rights of man", "one man one vote", and often gave a very frosty reception to any talk about the rights of women. Yet the reasons they gave for demanding personal freedom were quite general reasons, which could not be consistently halted at this point. And in discussing education, some of them—notably Rousseau—did recommend a good deal of freedom for "the child", provided always that that child was male. (See his Émile, *Of Education*, Book 5, for the quite different treatment of girls.)

All of this has given rise to plenty of ambivalence and confusion, not to say humbug. In our own day, however, exponents of "progressive" education have done good service by drawing out the full consequences of individualism for children both in theory and practice. What has emerged from these experiments is that some of it works and some does not. There are indeed many restraints that turn out to be unnecessary and harmful to children. But the attempt to suppress all restraints—to give the child a quite unstructured life, a blank slate on which it must creatively draw its own original picture of the world—is daft and doomed. Positive input is needed. Children need to have people around them who care enough about them to mind what they do and to give them guidance about it. They need a world-picture from which to start. They also need to know in some detail what they can expect from others, and what is actually going to be expected of them. (This is true even of adolescents who may often decide to reject that guidance and disappoint those expectations. Unless they know what the expectations are, their act will not have the meaning they intend.) If a child grew up surrounded by people who never expressed any views to it and never minded what it did—people who always answered "just as you please, dear" to any suggestion it might make—it could never orient itself in life at all.

Reflecting on this, we are likely, too, to wonder whether children are exceptional here. What about the rest of us? Would it be plausible to say that at a certain age—say sixteen, or eighteen, or twenty-one—we each become totally independent, and from that time on we design our own lives without any need for influence or direction from anybody around us? This is scarcely convincing. Even for adults, to live in a circle of people who never made any suggestion to us and always said "just as you like" to our own ideas would produce a deathly effect, not only chilling but deeply insulting. If everyone treated us like this, we would begin to protest, "why don't you take me seriously? Do you think I'm demented?" Painful though we often find the moral responses of others, we need them if we are to feel that we are alive at all. Moral solitude is an element in which our species can scarcely live, and that is true not just because of our weaknesses, but because of our strengths. Most of our capacities, both emotional and cerebral, are social ones. They fit us to do things along with others, and scrupulous isolation would make this impossible.

WHAT SORT OF LIFE, WHAT SORT OF HARM?

It is hard, then, to see how merely being allowed by others to live according to our own separate value-systems could give us a life of human fulfillment. "Allowing space" to other people is indeed necessary, but it can't mean withdrawing outside their lives altogether.

In these discussions of liberty, the need for us positively to help each other—and thereby to influence each other's lives —sometimes gets forgotten. No doubt it would be unfair to make too much of Brian Palmer's casual use of the cliché, "if you've got the money, honey". He was not being asked about his public duties but about the principles on which he conducted his personal life, and these may not have seemed to him to involve touching on how he would react to the claims of others outside his family. All the same, the topics are connected. If one thinks of duty to

others as being primarily a negative matter of respecting their privacy by
not interfering with them, one is certainly in some danger of not being
particularly watchful for occasions on which they need help.

This danger is not imaginary. There is in fact already an immense
difference in everyday neighbourly behaviour between those parts of the
modern world where a more traditional community-consciousness still
survives and some city areas where it has almost vanished—a difference
that can at times be vital to preserving a person's life and sanity. But
beyond this, there is the wider question of political duty, and here
individualism can run into a curious paradox. The liberties that we so much
prize in the West were won by campaigners who devoted their lives to
the cause of freedom, spending their own time and resources unsparingly
for this cause. If they had preferred to stay at home and do their own
thing, Mill and Shaftesbury, Wilberforce and Jefferson and Rousseau and
Mary Wollstonecraft and Tom Paine and hundreds of others would have
had a much easier and more pleasant life. Why did they not do so?

It is not plausible to say that fame and power repaid them. The
prospects of power were extremely remote, and the kind of fame involved
would not be valued by anybody who did not actually think this cause
important. What moved them, evidently, was not the direct desire to
enjoy "space" and freedom themselves, but a vision of a whole communal
way of life in which everybody could enjoy these things. They judged
this way of life to be so good that it was worthwhile to sacrifice their own
private interests to produce it. This is an example of a very important range
of value-judgements, which we all continually have to make, about ideals,
about the kind of life that we think is a good one. These judgements
determine the whole way in which our practical arrangements are structured, and they also do a great deal to determine what we count as harm.

For instance, from a traditional Hindu point of view, everything that
keeps people to the way of life that belongs to their caste is good, and
what might lead them to break away from it is harmful. From the Marxist
angle, all that makes for the revolution is good and what tends to postpone
it is therefore harmful. From a Freudian position, both these kinds of harm
are somewhat remote and unreal; what is really harmful is lack of self-
knowledge, though critics of Freudianism have sometimes suggested that
some limits to our self-knowledge may be necessary for our health and
sanity. Again, from the point of view of someone convinced of the

omnicompetence of science, any education or propaganda that might lower the standing of science is harmful.

This variation is not confined to sects or groups whom we might dismiss as extreme or eccentric. It appears everywhere in the way that resources are allocated. Societies that are devoted to a particular kind of art will give time and other resources to it that others might think should go to house-building, to religion, to money-making, to helping the poor or to promoting physical health. Societies valuing these arts will unhesitatingly see to it that their children spend the valuable time and attention of their most formative years on these arts, and will try to imbue them with a reverence for them that will tend to shape their whole lives.

In these societies, it will be considered deeply harmful to leave a child uneducated in the art that it will need for a full life. For instance, traditional Balinese culture demanded that everybody should dance, and modern Western culture demands that everybody shall read and do some elementary mathematics. Accordingly, to deprive anybody of these skills in these societies is to do them actual harm. All societies necessarily have such dominant values, and the attempt to remain impartial between them would lead only to a desperately impoverished existence. People have indeed sometimes entertained the idea that Western society is an exception to this rule, seeing it as an impartial spectator or judge, able to comprehend and evaluate all other civilisations. But this is an idle dream.

CONCLUSION: THE IMPORTANCE OF THE COMMUNAL

It follows that, in some sense and in some degree, each of us is constituted morally by our culture, by our society. In this chapter, we have been stressing this dependence—have been noting the necessary background of shared tradition that supports each of us and makes it possible for us to function morally in order to resist an unreal, over-isolated notion of the individual self. We have been looking at the communal aspect of morals, and that fact has been marked by the way in which, from time to time, we have been able to take certain moral judgements as examples that would plausibly be held in common.

I have cited a number of these examples, starting from Mill's own judgement about the superiority of free over automatic action, and the widely held objection to savage punishment, in the confident expectation that most of my readers would be likely, on reflection, to accept these views—not just arbitrarily or from habit, as they might declare a preference for tandoori over biriani, but because they cohere with very deep and general structures in the thought and life around us, structures that are built into all our lives.

That this confidence is not just arbitrary can be seen from a glance at what we would do if we do want to reject these judgements. If (for instance) we *disagree* with Mill about the superiority of free action, we do not just have to shout our disagreement and run off. We can argue, and if we are seriously interested we shall do so. Indeed, the behaviourist psychologist B.F. Skinner has done us all a service by starting an argument on this very point. He wrote a whole book *Beyond Freedom and Dignity* (Penguin, 1973) to question the value of these libertarian ideals and to insist that they have done a great deal of harm. In doing this, he gave reasons which the rest of us can weigh up and accept or reject. And in fact, this process goes on on a small scale all the time.

It is not true, though it is often said, that it is impossible to argue sensibly on moral topics. Every culture contains disagreements. Slight criticisms, slight discontents, are continually being expressed, and once they are expressed they can be further explained and intelligibly contested. Over time they can determine quite large changes of opinion. Any culture contains some materials for altering its own value-scheme, and with a very articulate, complex culture like ours, these materials are actually very abundant.

So far as this, the public, communal aspect of morals is evident, but how much further does it go? It is easy to see why, in argument within our own culture, we can rely on a shared background that gives both parties some common premises. But what happens when we travel outside that common culture? This we must explore in the next chapter.

11

Rethinking Relativism

THE PROBLEM OF CLASHING CUSTOMS

Is the difference between right and wrong perhaps really just determined by where you happen to live? Is morality perhaps always relative to culture, as manners and fashions are? Are all principles actually "valid only within their own frame of reference"?

This suspicion is an old and very natural one, and the Greeks were every bit as impressed by it as we are. I think it is worthwhile to start our discussion from the striking story that Herodotus used to illustrate it in the *Histories*. Though this story is well-known, it scarcely dates at all and it will lead us right into the heart of the problem. In Book III, ch.38 we read:

> When Darius was king of Persia, he summoned the Greeks who happened to be present at his court, and asked them what they would take to eat the dead bodies of their fathers. They replied that they would not do it for any money in the world. Later, in the presence of the Greeks, and through an interpreter (so that they could understand what was said), he asked some Indians, of the tribe called Callatiae, who do in fact eat their parents' dead bodies, what they would take to burn them. They uttered a cry of horror, and forbade him to mention such a dreadful thing. One can see by this what custom can do, and Pindar, in my opinion, was right when he called it "king of all".

When I say that this story does not date, I mean that we could at once parallel the kind of situation Herodotus describes from items in any day's newspaper. We who are not kings certainly cannot often bring together so neatly both parties to these disagreements. But because cultures are so freely mixed together today, profound, painful disagreements of this sort continually take place. People are constantly being confronted with each other's customs and exclaiming that it would be simply unthinkable for any decent person to accept them.

Yet there has also been an important change. The mere fact that these clashes are now so common means that in another way things are now radically altered. Nearly all of us today know that people with quite different customs from our own do exist. The communication explosion has meant that virtually everybody, even in quite remote corners of the world, now grows up with the background knowledge that there are many ways of life deeply different from their own—a kind of knowledge which used once to be quite rare.

THE SACREDNESS OF CUSTOM

This different context actually makes a great change in the nature of the problem, a change which we must consider shortly. But first, it is important to notice that the horrified reaction reported by Herodotus is not just mindless prejudice. Respect for custom is not pathological; it is normal, not only to our own species, but to most intelligent animals. A relatively fixed background of custom is necessary as the base on which an enterprising, constructive, complex way of life is to be built. Forms that we grow up with—manners, ceremonies, festivals, clothes, kinds of food and drink, social habits, shared concerns and fears and jokes and venerations and inhibitions—enter deeply into our being.

CONFORMITY AND FASHION

If anyone doubts this need, it may be worthwhile to notice the immense concern that many people feel today about the details of correct fashionable clothing—a concern that can go deep even with people who particularly pride themselves on being emancipated from tradition. The right shirts, the right jeans and trainers and hair-do are absolutely obligatory, and though fashion constantly changes the details of what is right, the general demand to keep up with fashion is still a strong, unchanging, external one, imposed on individuals by the group. A number of people have been murdered (it is said) in America recently, merely for the sake of their fashionable training-shoes. If, in fact, a ruler today were to ask the same question that Darius asked, "What would you take to dress unfashionably for a year?" it seems likely that many people would give him the same kind of answer that Darius got from the Greeks and Callatiae.

Mill, indeed, noted this interesting change, which was already becoming marked in his day, from conformity with the past to conformity within the present moment:

> We have discarded the fixed costumes of our forefathers; everyone must still dress like other people, but the fashion may change once or twice a year. We thus take care that when there is a change, it shall be for change's sake, and not from any idea of beauty or convenience; for the same idea of beauty or convenience would not strike all the world at the same moment.
>
> (Liberty, p.128)

I mention this example, not to sneer at fashion, but because it may save us from the misleading impression, which we very easily get, that we, as modern people, are exempt from the bonds of custom. Because we hear of so many cultures—because we are so much better informed about diversity than people used to be—we may feel that we have moved onto a different plane and are looking straight past all these symbols at the reality, which we alone can see. If we think that, then our relativism is entirely a view about the customs of *other people*. And that means that we have not begun to see the real problem.

SYMBOL AND MEANING

Why are the demands of custom so strong? Why, when details of clothing or even burial rites might seem quite a superficial matter, are they things for which people are prepared to die at times? Evidently, surface details like these become the symbolic vessels in which meanings of the first importance are carried, and these meanings cannot easily be transferred without being spilt. Like the Greeks and the Callatiae in Herodotus' story, the devotees of sharp dressing identify the symbols closely with the values that they symbolise, and do not feel it possible to have the one without the other.

Is the meaning something separate that can exist without this clothing? In a sense it must be so, because the same meaning often seems to appear in many different clothings. When we hear of an astonishing custom, our first thought, after getting over our surprise, is to ask what deeper, more or less universal meaning, intelligible in principle to ourselves, lies hidden behind this strange symbol. This is a constant question with travellers and anthropologists, and very often it gets a clear answer. Thus we see at once that a common respect for the dead underlies equally the customs of both the Greeks and the Callatiae. We regularly assume that some such meaning is present, as readily as we assume that people talking a strange language are not simply babbling but have got some meaning to their words—a meaning that, given favourable circumstances, would convey something to us too.

This assumption is not just an optimistic fancy. It is a necessary condition of our practical condition. If we did not have, at some level, a common mental structure with other people, we could not live with them at all, and we rightly assume that, in spite of their diversity, in principle, strangers are people with whom it is eventually possible to live. We do not have to assume that they are in any way just like us, but we do have to assume, if we are to communicate with them at all, that there is an adequate likeness in basic structure. This is part of our general assumption of inhabiting a single world which is in principle coherent and intelligible—an assumption that is needed as much for science as for morals, and is indeed the basis of all thought. We will come back to this important assumption at the end of the chapter.

Thus we rightly assume that in most cases the custom has a meaning that is accessible to us too. But that meaning is not necessarily something perfectly definite that can be stated clearly apart from the custom as a body can be undressed. Both Greeks and Callatiae saw their particular ways of treating the dead as the only possible ways of expressing due respect, and what the two groups meant by that respect may not have been widely different. Yet there will have been some differences in the kind of respect, because the two sets of symbols would not have been chosen had they not grown out of different background lives and values, and once the symbols were chosen, they would affect the meaning that was understood to lie beneath them.

Meanings and symbols do normally develop together and change together. When it becomes necessary to change customs—as of course it often does—there is always a problem about transferring the old meanings to new vessels, or, on occasion, about deliberately dropping parts of that meaning and incorporating new elements. The choice of a particular symbol sometimes does very important work, and the exact point of that work is not always obvious or known. That, indeed, is why it is healthy and reasonable to feel a certain reluctance about changing symbols. Though we often have reason to criticise existing customs, their relative fixedness does guard the continuity of our own characters, and it also supplies the language in which we communicate with each other. These forms are not just arbitrary empty shells; they shape the structures round which the meaning of our lives evolves. Because of what they contain and convey, we are right to treat them as precious, indeed as sacred. That is why the communal aspect of morality is so important, and it is why there is indeed a serious core of truth in relativism

PLURALITY AND TOLERANCE

But we have to sort out this reasonable relativism from other ideas that make no sense. Custom alone cannot really be king of all in the sense of being an absolute despot, though people often try to make it so. That would exclude all change and leave us helpless in the face of variety. The impression of sacredness must not be treated as absolute, for several reasons.

First, that impression cannot tell us what to do when we want to make changes in our own culture. For instance, cruel sports such as gladiatorial games and bear-baiting have often had great symbolic importance within particular societies, such as Rome and 16th-century England. But those societies abolished them in the end because they thought them cruel. In doing so, they showed their wish to change, not just these particular activities, but also their own symbolic commitment. They showed their wish to become less cruel societies.

Again, the sense of sacredness attaching to our own habits cannot help us when we have to deal with outsiders who are equally committed to the sacredness of something different. People who meet these clashes for the first time are inclined simply to be bewildered and incredulous, like Herodotus' Callatiae. They will not themselves conform to the strange custom, and they often feel that they cannot even go on living in the same world with the bizarre alien beings who accept it. They may try to put the custom down by force. This, however, is liable to produce wars, persecutions, oppressive laws and great problems of policing even if you win, and there is always the awkward possibility that you might lose. Persuasion can be tried, but it often fails. Accordingly, many people and many governments in the modern world have drifted into an uncertain policy of live-and-let-live, of tolerating diverse customs and moral views in practice so long as they do not lead to violent mutual interference.

Considered simply as a practice, this has obviously a great deal to recommend it. But there still remains an underlying dilemma. If we take this tolerant stand, are we saying that the alien practices are in fact all right, or merely that they are wrong but that we do not see how to stop them? The second alternative is disturbing; it seems to convict us of feebleness and lack of courage. The first is also disturbing, because it suggests that perhaps we ourselves ought to change, or at least that our existing habits are less certainly superior than we thought.

Accordingly, people usually avoid this dilemma by a compromise which says something more modest like "to each his own. Customs and moral beliefs are valid within the cultures to which they belong, but they have no validity outside them". This compromise may be called simple, confident relativism.

SIMPLE RELATIVISM

That sounds good, but what does the compromise-formula mean? What, in particular, does the confident word "valid" mean? The compromise seems to commit us to saying positively that the existing principles of other cultures *are valid in those cultures*. But this is making a judgement about something internal to those cultures. How are we, as outsiders, in any position to do that? For instance: if we, who live in society X, are confronted with an alien society Y, which approves of something contrary to our mores, such as ritual murder or mutilation or child prostitution or polygamy or public drunkenness or football on Sunday, the simple relativist stance clearly forbids us to say that these practices are *wrong*. But does it allow us to say that they are right? If a few rebellious individuals inside society Y start to question these customs, are we committed to saying that they ought not to do so, because each morality is valid on its own territory? If we are not, it is hard to see that our endorsement of its validity meant much.

Again, suppose that the members of yet a third society Z intervene, expressing their own violent disapproval of ritual murder or Sunday football, and try to stop it. Are we now entitled—or perhaps even obliged—to resist them, on the grounds that they are interfering with something that is locally valid? Or do our principles rather call on us to leave the Zians alone, since they are only following the principles of their own society, which in any case may not share our relativist principle of tolerance?

Lastly too, what about possible reforms that we might want to make in our own society? Are these changes ruled out by the fact that the customs we have now are locally valid and must not be changed? Or do the new principles perhaps become valid themselves at the point where the majority begins to accept them—thus bearing out the suggestion which Hobbes seems to have made (and which governments usually follow), that rebellion is only wrong while it is unsuccessful, and becomes right on the day when it succeeds.

SCEPTICAL RELATIVISM

When questions are as maddening as this, it is reasonable to suspect that they ought not to arise at all, that something has gone wrong if we are having to ask them. But these questions often do arise today, because attempts at simple relativism are constantly being made. These are not just perverse, nit-picking, academic questions. They result from the over-confident sweepingness of the simple relativist principle, which in cases of conflict apparently calls on us to endorse two or more incompatible sets of principles as valid at the same time. Since this can't be done, that simple principle is often diluted to a weaker form, which may be called Negative, Sceptical or Fatalistic Relativism. This holds simply that nobody can say anything valid about moral questions in cultures other than their own. It has no view about whether people *can* do this difficult thing inside their own culture. And its message, in the case just mentioned, seems to be that we must not interfere either with the Yians or the Zians, but must leave them to stew in their own respective juices.

Why is valid moral thinking about other cultures, and perhaps also about one's own, impossible in this way? Is it because of our ignorance? Or is it because there are moral objections to interfering? Here again, both moral and epistemological reasons can be given, and we commonly find a mixture of both. They must be separated, and again, I believe that the moral set are much the more pressing of the two. Again, too, I think that they arise largely from concentration on one very important but peculiar set of examples—namely here, ones involving imperialism. It will probably, therefore, be best to begin by looking directly at this special and rather murky example.

THE IMPERIALIST MODEL

Empires are, of course, a context where this problem of clashing moralities easily arises. They may even be the place where it first arose in any serious form. If we suppose that there was (roughly speaking) an ancient primitive state where distinct groups of hunter-gatherers were living side by side without any one group's attempting to rule the others, we can see that their moralities would not often have occasion to clash. But if one people starts to conquer and rule the rest, then conformity begins to be expected, and this is when serious trouble can start. It is interesting that Herodotus' story has this setting. The Persian King appears there in the role of the detached, sophisticated, neutral observer above the dispute who understands other people's difficulties. He is the one who can see through the superficial symbols to the reality behind them. The Persians, after all, neither burned their own dead nor ate them. They knew very well that they had solved the problem of disposal in the only *right* way, namely by putting corpses on high towers and letting the vultures eat them.

From this outside, superior point of view, the customs of various subject peoples can appear simply as different behaviour-patterns to be studied and fitted into one's own plans in the most convenient way. It is often good sense for rulers not to object to anything their subjects do that does not endanger order, but to make their officials treat even the most eccentric customs with respect. Indeed, the reason why Herodotus cites this story is to back his suggestion that another king, Cambyses, who did deliberately violate the temples of his subject peoples, must have been mad.

JUDGEMENT IS NOT INTERFERENCE

This convenient, pragmatic tolerance, however, tells us nothing about the boundaries of valid judgement. Those boundaries simply do not come into question until we start to think about clashes that involve our own morality. That is when, for the first time, a moral issue arises. When this happens, imperial powers often put their foot down, as the British did in India over suttee, the Russians in Eastern Europe over attempts to spread Christian propaganda, and the Americans in various countries over attempts to spread Marxism.

Is this interference necessarily objectionable? One reason for objecting to it is, of course, a general objection to empire as such, or indeed a wider, more anarchistic objection to all government. We may say that societies should be governed only by rulers of their own choosing, or that they should not have rulers at all. This will then be a reason for saying that the British, Russians or Americans had no business to be ruling over people outside their own society in the first place, and we may well be right about this.

But this objection to certain kinds of political action carries no implication at all about the possibility of moral judgement. All of us, including colonial officials themselves, are often in positions where we cannot *act* on our judgements, but this does not mean that we cannot judge validly. Very many perfectly sensible moral judgements that are made are ones that cannot be acted on. Powerless people can quite properly judge those in power. We constantly judge the dead, or remote living people who are outside our control for various reasons. We even judge imaginary people in books. For instance, a colonial official who gets instructions from the government to ignore and tolerate something like suttee or child prostitution is in no way barred by this from continuing to think about the question of whether this practice is wrong.

THE USE OF LIMITED SCEPTICISM

We need to keep epistemological questions—questions about the possibility of validly judging such cases—quite distinct from moral questions about the legitimacy of empire. About that legitimacy, many of us have formed, and can confidently express, strong and definite moral judgements. Over these judgements we are usually not at all sceptical or hesitant, even when the empires in question are not our own. About the general possibility of judging other cultures validly, however, we do at times become hesitant and sceptical—incredulous—and that scepticism is brought in, sometimes reasonably, sometimes not, to back our objections to empire.

One obviously reasonable and limited use of scepticism is where the acts of imperial rulers show ignorance of detailed facts about the communities they rule. This seems often to have happened, especially about religious and marital customs. It is indeed almost incredible with what naive over-confidence Europeans have often crashed in to change the customs of the countries they invaded. A good example of that over-confidence is the way in which people in many Third World countries have been induced to become dependent on cash crops for export by rulers who simply did not understand the workings of the complex and well-adapted indigenous economies that were thus destroyed. It is reasonable enough that we have now reacted to become extremely hesitant, extremely uncertain whether we know the facts well enough to criticise other cultures. But the ignorance we are concerned with here is factual ignorance of an ordinary, specific kind. It is not some universal, metaphysical kind of ignorance affecting everything moral.

NOTES

About relativism and the plurality of cultures, a very good source is still *Patterns of Culture* by Ruth Benedict, (London, Routledge and Kegan Paul, 1935). Also *New Lives for Old* (London, Gollancz, 1956), a late book by Margaret Mead, in which she corrected the over-simple relativist emphasis of her early work. See also "On Trying Out One's New Sword" in my *Heart and Mind*, (London, Methuen Paperback, 1980).

About human universals, see *The Tangled Wing, Biological Constraints on the Human Spirit*, by Melvin Konner (London, Heinemann, 1982). Also my *Beast and Man, The Roots of Human Nature* (London, Methuen Paperback, 1980).

12

How Large Is a Culture?

CAN OTHERS JUDGE US?

How, then, should we deal with the big questions which certainly do arise about the possibility of mutual understanding among different sorts of societies? It may be best to start by moving right away from the hypnotic case of empire, and looking at a quite different set of examples. Let us try simply reversing the position, and asking whether our own culture can be validly judged by those outside it. If (for instance) Japanese or Papuan or Kenyan or Russian critics mention something about our society which they think wrong, ought we to tell them that their comments are invalid because they don't know what they are talking about?

It is not obvious what could justify us in making this rather disrespectful response. Moreover, if we did make it, we would obviously lose a mass of suggestions that have proved extremely valuable. It is interesting to notice how, during the early Enlightenment, new and effective social criticism was often expressed by exploiting just this situation. In books like Montesquieu's *Persian Letters*, Goldsmith's *Letters from John Chinaman*, Swift's *Gulliver's Travels* and many other successful satires, acute authors gave great force to their own comments by writing them as if they were reported criticisms from remote cultures. This was possible because travel books were already beginning to report real criticisms of this kind, and the device was very effective. Readers did not react by protesting that all this criticism—both from the real travel books and from the spoofs—was invalid because it came, or was supposed to come, from people who knew very little of European society. They took the books very seriously. They saw the supposedly external origin of the complaints not as a disqualification, but as giving them extra force. They certainly did not see it as ground for denying the validity of the comments.

Were these readers wrong in their response? Ought they to have been more incredulous? They could, of course, rightly have complained about mistakes of detail, arguing that certain parts of the criticism showed ignorance of particular facts. Thus, when the rational horses in the last chapter of *Gulliver's Travels* respond with puzzled distaste to all Gulliver's reports of personal affection and partiality among human beings, or when the King of Brobdingnag expresses his utter disgust at human modes of government, readers might wish to defend their own species by mentioning certain facts about its psychological constitution. Indeed, part of the point of these satires is to make us look for such defences and see how sound they are. *But these are detailed points*, and the kind of defence that can be made against them depends on being able to show that the facts actually are different from what the critic supposed. It is no sort of defence simply to point out that this critic is an outsider.

CULTURES ARE NOT MONOLITHS

A very important question comes in sight here. What makes someone an outsider? How wide, in fact, are the borders of a culture?

We have to ask these questions when we realise that we do not feel in the least justified in rejecting the comments of outside critics simply because they are outsiders. When we reflect on their position in the way just suggested, we often see that we have to take their ideas very seriously. This should surely make us begin to wonder whether they are indeed as completely outside our culture as we had supposed. Does not *any* acquaintance with a culture bring one in some degree inside it—perhaps far enough inside it to make useful moral criticisms? If these critics have visited our society, or have had some experience of dealing with our countrymen abroad, or have read a good deal about us, or have even just heard one of us describe how we live (like the King of Brobdingnag), then there is surely nothing in principle to prevent their comments from being worth hearing. Any general, comprehensive scepticism about the possibility of their being relevant would be bizarre and offensive.

This suggests something still more crucial for the program of relativism. *There is no watertight boundary around a culture,* marking off a set of people who are licensed to talk about it validly from the rest who are not. Instead, there is a great variety of positions, both outside and inside any society, from which different aspects of it can be seen. There are always people with a foot in more than one society, such as traders, exiles and travellers. There are officials regulating affairs for those people. There are cross-cultural partnerships and mixed marriages, producing bilingual children. There are exchanges of objects such as clothes, tools and pottery as well as of pictures, music and other expressive artefacts. There are also sometimes direct political transactions.

Obviously the kind of understanding that results from these various proceedings varies greatly with the different kind of relations involved, and also with the sensibilities of particular observers. But then that is also true of the understanding that insiders have of their own culture. Merely belonging to a culture is not enough to make one automatically able to understand it morally. The society's own members vary endlessly in the kind of opportunities, powers and motives that they have for understanding it, and so do outsiders. Nobody is infallible; and for that reason many different points of view are needed. The degree of authority with which they can speak will naturally vary with the kind of topic they are talking about and with the range and quality of their own experience—exactly as happens with inside members of the society too.

However, there is also a special kind of force possessed by a genuinely outside comment, a stranger's astonished response to the bare report of how we live. This astonishment is what often does the work in *Gulliver's Travels,* and for this purpose the fact that the commentators are imaginary does not much matter. Their fictitiousness does not prevent their remarks from having a terrible force. Of course real examples have a special force of their own. A painful recent example has been the astonishment with which many people from simpler cultures have responded to such things as hearing how old people are treated in the West. The astonishment itself is what we need to hear, and genuine outsiders can present it with still more force than imaginary ones.

WHO ARE OUTSIDERS?

Thus even those who seem to be genuine outsiders—even people who are hearing about us for the first time—can make moral comments about us which we recognise as valid. But when we begin to ask where the borderline of these genuine outsiders should be drawn and where people who are in some sense members of our society begin, we see how unrealistic the whole picture of isolated, watertight cultures has been. Cultures do differ, but they differ in a way which is much more like that of climatic regions or ecosystems than it is like the frontiers drawn with a pen between nation states. They shade into one another. And in our own day there is such a continuous and all-pervading cultural interchange that the idea of separateness holds no water at all.

This mixed and interdependent condition, though it has lately been much intensified, is not new. If we go back in our own history a little, we see that what we might think of as a single modern Western culture has been built up out of endless contribution from Greeks, Jews, Romans, Celts, Germans, and in later years from practically every country in the world, and still contains a rich confusion of uncombined elements from all these sources. These ancestral societies too were themselves built up from their own varying sources, and were in their time complex and subject to constant change. There has never been a primitive condition of genuine separateness, a basic human model of complete divergence from which we might suppose ourselves to be deviating. The idea of separate social monoliths is utterly unreal and unhistorical.

We might ask too whether, even within our own epoch, we want to regard Western culture as a single unit, or as a loose cluster, and how far its ramifications extend? There are important cultural differences even within a country the size of Britain, let alone within one like Russia or India or the United States. Even within Scotland, the Western Isles rightly refuse to be identified with Glasgow. It is sometimes useful to talk of sub-cultures, but at what level are they supposed to start? All these questions are a terrible headache for any attempt to map out a consistent doctrine of relativism.

THE DEEPER UNITY

Thus every human society that we know of has some interaction with others. Everywhere people wander and trade and ask questions about each other and learn from outsiders. And underlying this habit there is the still more important background presupposition of a unity beneath the divergence. In spite of their differences, people do tend to suppose that at a profound level the human race is in some way one, that its basic moral structure is universal. This belief emerges in the appeal that people everywhere make to their common humanity when outsiders attack them. It emerges from the very widespread idea that surface diversity may conceal a common message—as when we read the difference between burning and eating the dead as essentially just a difference between two ways of expressing a shared attitude of respect for them. It emerges from the way in which people everywhere are inclined to say that those who practise customs that they abominate are not really human at all but are "animals". Perhaps most significant of all, it emerges when those who want to change their customs look for other and deeper standards to appeal to—when they criticise existing morality on the grounds that it is not what the underlying nature of humanity demands.

This assumption of a real moral unity, a common human nature, has been taken for granted during most of the history of our society, as indeed of most others and, as I have just suggested, it is still unofficially taken for granted in much of our thinking today. It is also supported by a great mass of evidence, both from history and from anthropology, of actual moral similarities between different cultures. However, this idea has been brought into some disrepute by theorists who have repeatedly hijacked it to lend force to oppressive political ideas. Institutions such as slavery, war, inequality of civic rights and the general subjection of women have often been defended as being expressions of this timeless, unchangeable human nature. More generally, too, it was claimed that other existing customs cannot be changed because they are linked to that timeless human nature. For theorists of this kind, "human nature" has effectively often meant the *status quo* in their own society.

It is not surprising, then, that reformers attacking these institutions have at times responded, not just by pointing out that these defenders of oppression had got human nature wrong, but by claiming that there was no such thing as human nature at all. In the last three centuries (starting roughly from the empiricist manifestos of John Locke), they have developed this view into a claim which is itself a very startling theory of human nature—a special view of what human beings are really like. This claim is that human beings are originally colourless, neutral stuff, standard items, "blank paper at birth", putty, which is infinitely malleable in the hands of educators. This means that any change is possible, so the inertia of custom need never be respected. It means too that any individual can, if properly educated, do as well as any other, which looks like a useful argument on behalf of equality of opportunity.

This project of cutting out the whole idea of human nature is, I think, another striking example of an idea understandably taken up for strong and reputable moral reasons, but stretched to do much wider work beyond its capacity. It is a classic case of curing a cold by cutting off your head. The proper response to institutions stained with racism, sexism and other forms of political oppression is to say just what is wrong with them and to point out means by which they can in fact be changed. It is no use trying to shortcut this work by making the wild claim that human beings are infinitely malleable, blank paper at birth—a suggestion that cannot be believed by anyone who has ever seen a baby. That there is *some* underlying human nature—some basic structure indicating what kinds of things can be good and bad for human beings—is a perfectly harmless assumption that we all need to make, and constantly do make, for all kinds of purposes. (I have discussed its meaning, and the kinds of objection that can be made to it, more fully in my book *Beast and Man*.) The real source of trouble is the quite different assumption that our own preferred customs are the only ones which suit this nature. That (as Herodotus pointed out) is something people tend to think, but they have to learn better.

SOURCES OF THE MONOLITH MYTH

(1) Anthropology

It is worth asking why we have been led to underestimate so surprisingly this continuity and underlying unity that links cultures, and to build up the misleading model of them as being radically separate. Again, the reasons seem largely to have been moral, and to have been respectable in themselves, but unduly one-sided.

Early enquirers about non-European cultures tended to exaggerate the ways in which these societies differed from European models, partly from sensationalism, but partly also in order to show these people as independent and worthy of study, rather than just as standard "savages" or inferior imitators. Early anthropologists, when they formalised these studies, deepened this tendency, both from this same moral motive, and also for scientific convenience. They wanted to inspect their phenomena in as pure a state as possible. They therefore deliberately chose for their studies isolated groups of "tribes" who would be uncontaminated by Western civilisation, and would also be as free as possible from confusing influences from neighbouring peoples. It is now recognised that this approach produced a misleading bias, and anthropologists today try to correct it by taking on their enormous subject in all its real complexity.

(2) Unreal Histories

Another confusing factor, less obvious but possibly deeper, has been the rather widespread habit that particular nations everywhere have had of simplifying and dramatising their own history. They tend to do this by constructing myths that show their own people as a pure group, descended from a single ancestor who lived at or soon after the time when the human race was created, and whose fortunes determined their distinct cultural heritage at that time for ever. These myths have a function in unifying the group imaginatively—in reinforcing its pride and sense of separateness—and also in making those customs the myth describes look sacred and unchangeable. Hesiod provided the Greeks with this sort of bond-forming ancestral background in his *Theogony*, and the writers of the Book of Genesis did it for the Jews.

In both these cases the history of the stories themselves is important. They are by no means just simple, primitive oral traditions. (The Book of Genesis is not even one of the earlier books in the Bible.) Though the basic myths may well be older, both Hesiod's genealogies and the Book of Genesis are deliberate, quite sophisticated retellings of those stories, from a definite political angle, retellings that are meant to support particular views about the special value and function of their nations, and to emphasise in certain ways their separateness from the other nations around them. Thus in Genesis, when God accepts the offerings of Abel the pastoralist and rejects those of Cain the agriculturalist, the moral is meant to strengthen the Israelites in their nomadic, pastoral way of life, to discourage them from lapsing into settled agriculture (as they constantly tended to do). It also serves to justify their hostility to the settled people round them who were deemed to be children of Cain. The myth-maker is an active propagandist.

As things turned out, this symbolic function of these stories did have value in giving both these peoples a sense of their peculiar destiny and mission. However in both cases it also had some bad consequences in making them despise their neighbours. And even apart from this drawback, the symbolic function is quite a separate thing from historical truth. Serious historical investigation of the kind now possible is a different kind of enterprise from myth-making. To make myths is to express through symbols one's most profound, fundamental value-judgements and also one's most general metaphysical beliefs—beliefs about how the world is basically constituted. Although particular historical facts are often used in this symbolism, the historical correctness of those facts does not normally matter at all.

This is important in the example of Genesis, because it affects our own culture. It became clear quite early in the 19th century (well before Darwin) that an immense range of facts emerging about geology made it no longer possible for any impartial person to suppose that the world had been created at the time suggested in the Book of Genesis—that is, between four and six thousand years before our own day. It had to be enormously older. This discovery affects the historical accuracy of most creation-myths in other cultures too, since most of them, except perhaps Hinduism, also give the world much too recent an origin.

The point of myths, however, does not lie in their historical accuracy but in their spiritual message. Often that message is of immense value, a value which remains quite unaffected and undamaged by a changed understanding of the historical details, but these creation-myths often have the other much less respectable aspect. They are used for the exclusive exaltation of one particular nation by giving it a special place at the creation, and also to tie it to a certain fixed set of customs, which is said to have been instituted then. The myths exploit the authority of their apparent antiquity to teach chauvinism and conformism.

We may perhaps find it easier to shake off these malign messages if we once grasp that the story is in any case unhistorical, and was never intended to be historical in the modern sense. For instance, the separate origins alleged by the myths can often be disproved simply by noting that peoples who are now distant from each other, and admit no kinship, show close similarities of language and culture, which prove beyond question that they had a common origin in a time far more distant than any contemplated in the myths. Human history turns out to be both far longer and far richer, far more complicated than the myth-makers ever imagined. We are all members one of another to an extent that shows up cultural chauvinism as a mean, barren, foolish and unrealistic dream.

CONCLUSION: THE USES AND LIMITATIONS OF RELATIVISM

I have been mentioning some reasons why the idea of separate, monolithic societies, each with its own quite separate morality, is unrealistic. I have suggested that this notion has gained most of its power and popularity from being useful as a weapon against cultural imperialism. I have suggested too that it is not a satisfactory tool to use for this very important purpose. It does not really make sense. Its apparent sweepingness is illusory in a way that becomes obvious once we move away from the example of imperialism and try to apply it to a different range of cases. Its imposing pretensions are just another instance of false universality.

Any principle that invalidates all moral thinking about one society by those outside it would exempt imperialists themselves, as well as everybody else, from much-needed criticism. Today, no thoughtful person is likely to claim this immunity. Societies are now too obviously mixed and open to one another for it to seem plausible that any group has the last word and can shrug off all outside critics. But that is what even the most modest and sceptical form of systematic relativism would demand.

This does not mean that relativism has been a pointless doctrine. As I suggested earlier, its emphasis on the public aspect of morals—on the absolute need that individuals have for the background of a coherent society—is an essential element in understanding how moralities work. We do need relatively stable, corporate ways of life, and our value-judgements do take shapes made possible by our societies. The respect for these symbolic forms which we express when we criticise imperialists for overriding them is justified. But when we look away from these remoter cases to others nearer home, we see that this respect cannot be absolute. It is not the only consideration involved. Morality demands a wider horizon of possibilities than any existing society can supply. It is not just a matter of customs but of spiritual insights and ideals. Its field of reference is the world.

Because relativism has these weaknesses, it is usually invoked only for a certain range of cases, most of them political. It is when people are thinking about the relations between groups—especially when they are confronted by the spectacle of a powerful group interfering with the customs of a weaker one—that they tend to claim that each morality is valid only within its own group. A great many moral questions, however, do not concern relations between groups, but those between individuals. Here the kinds of moral scepticism that are popular today tend to take a different, more individualistic form. They choose a much smaller moral unit. Instead of claiming that each morality is valid only in its own group, they prefer to say that each is valid only for a single individual, that each person creates a private set of values and standards by individual decision. This is subjectivism, and we must discuss it in the next chapter.

NOTES

Empiricism is the idea that all knowledge derives from experience, rather than either from any outside authority or from principles which need to be learnt. As Locke put it in his *Essay Concerning Human Understanding* (1690), "The senses at first let in particular ideas, and furnish the yet empty cabinet", "Let us suppose the mind to be, as we say white paper ... how comes it to be furnished?" Locke's simple answer "experience" looks plausible till you come to ask how experience itself could take place at all if the growing organism had no particular capacities or motives of its own—no principles of selection among the data that pour in on it. The dispute between empiricists and rationalists—who give a corresponding primacy to reason over experience—is really a rivalry of exaggerations. Both doctrines are half-truths.

13

Varieties of Subjectivism

SPECIMENS—THE SOUND OF TRUMPETS

What is subjectivism? Let us start with a few declarations:

(1) There needeth an holy yea-saying; its own will the spirit now willeth; he that was lost to the world gaineth his own world...Once you said "God" when you gazed on distant seas, but now I have taught you to say "superman". God is a supposition, but I want your supposing to reach no further than your creating will. Could you create a God? So be silent about all gods. But you could surely create the superman.

> (Nietzsche, *Thus Spake Zarathustra*, "In the Happly Isles")

(2) None yet knoweth what is good or evil—unless it be that he is a creator!

But a creator is he that *createth man's goal* and giveth earth its meaning and its future; he it is that first maketh good and evil *to be*.

> (Nietzsche, *Thus Spake Zarathustra*, "Of Old and New Tables")

(3) "My judgement is my judgement, to which hardly anyone else has a right", is what the philosopher of the future will say. One must get rid of the bad taste of wishing to agree with many others. "Good" is no longer good in the mouth of my neighbour. And how could there be a "common good?" The expression contradicts itself; what can be common cannot have much value.

> (Nietzsche, *Beyond Good and Evil*, 2nd article, section 43)

(4) You are free, therefore choose—that is to say, invent. No rule of general morality can show you what you ought to do; no signs are vouchsafed in this world.

(Jean-Paul Sartre, *Existentialism and Humanism*, p. 38)

(5) It is nowhere written that "the good" exists, that one must be honest or must not lie, since we are now upon the plane where there are only men. Dostoevsky once wrote, "If God did not exist, everything would be permitted"; and that, for Existentialism, is the starting-point.

(Jean-Paul Sartre, ibid., p. 32-3)

(6) [Answering the objection "your values are not serious, since you choose them yourself"]—To that I can only say that I am very sorry that it should be so; but if I have excluded God the father, there must be somebody to invent values.

(Jean-Paul Sartre, ibid., p. 54)

(7) Many words have been granted me, and some are wise, and some are false, but only three are holy; "I will it!"... Whatever road I take, the guiding star is within me; the guiding star and the lodestone which point the way. They point in but one direction. They point to me.

(Ayn Rand, *The Anthem*, p. 109)

(8) There is nothing to take a man's freedom away from him, save other men. To be free, a man must be free of his brothers. That is freedom. That and nothing else.

(Ayn Rand, ibid., p. 119)

(9) I tend to operate on the assumption that what I want to do and what I feel like is what I should do. What I think the universe wants from me is to take my values, whatever they might happen to be, and live up to them as much as I can.

(Margaret Oldham, *Habits of the Heart*, ed. Bellah, p. 14)

(10) Life is a big pinball game and you have to be able to move and adjust yourself to situations if you're going to enjoy it... I've always loved that thing that Mark Twain said about something being moral is something you feel

good after and something immoral is something you feel bad after. Which implies that you got to try everything at least once.

(Ted Oster, ibid., p. 77)

THE LONE CREATOR

These voices are of course not all saying the same thing. There are deep differences between them, and some of them also have internal conflicts. We must attend to these differences in a moment. It is a central and by now familiar theme of this book that entirely distinct doctrines are often jumbled together and held as a whole to satisfy conflicting demands. But in spite of the differences it is worthwhile to start by noticing what these voices have in common.

First, all these passages agree in saying that individuals can get no moral guidance from outside. They all put forward the claim that moral decisions depend solely on choices which each person must make quite alone. The unit of morality has contracted. The point here is no longer—as with relativism—that moral views are valid only within a given culture, but that they are so only within a given single life. Each person must invent or create them from scratch.

Practically speaking, this would be a change of earth-shaking importance. In ordinary life we have drawn most of what we think from those around us, and we expect to go on learning all the time from other people on moral matters. We pool our experience. The people whom we admire influence us greatly, and we are in no doubt that they ought to. We take their principles very seriously. Normally, too, we treat with considerable respect even views that are accepted by most people in our culture. Relativism approves this habit, indeed exalts it into an absolute principle. Subjectivism, by contrast, drops it altogether. There is no way in which these two doctrines can be combined.

As with many other clashes between extreme views, it seems likely that both these simple views are overstated and need to be rethought in more realistic forms. Both have arisen, in fact, as correctives for certain particular kinds of error, and each has then been inflated by a false assumption of universality and represented as a guiding principle for the whole of life. This simple rhetoric of extremes has great power in a desperately confusing world. Extreme philosophers are, after all, much the easiest to read, and generally the only ones who get widely read at all.

What is still more unlucky, however, is that the rhetoric of these two opposite and incompatible extremes is so similar that people often do not distinguish between them. Relativism and subjectivism tend to be used together as constituting a muddled, composite kind of immoralism, a secure "modern" and enlightened way of doing without traditional morals. The brute incompatibility between the two approaches is largely disguised by using them for different kinds of cases. Relativism is used for talking about other people's cultures, ("they have a right to their own way of life"); subjectivism for talking about one's own.

This division of labour probably shows which way the wind is really blowing. Disputes within our own society are real to us, and about these disputes we, as "modern" people, seldom if ever take the simple relativist line that morality is entirely determined by culture, so that dissenting individuals must of course be in the wrong. Nor would we really expect dissenting individuals within other cultures to be bound by that principle either.

There are some outstanding cases, such as the oppression of women in certain non-Western cultures, notably in extreme cases of practices like clitoridectomy, where a contented relativist acceptance would shock the contemporary conscience fairly severely. In theory at least, we take conscientious objection to this and many other practices very seriously, and we mostly accept a good deal of the case that Mill presented for freedom of thought and speech. Relativism cannot satisfy that case. It is only an early way-station on the path towards greater freedom. In a world where cultures are all the time becoming less separate, more interconnected, it gets less and less adequate. The difficulties that we saw in it in the last chapter point us firmly on to the next stage of that path.

THE PROBLEM OF PRIVATE VALIDITY

But what will that stage be? Is it possible to be really free while remaining subject to morality at all? Here we must notice another striking point common to most of the quotations just given. All of them—except, significantly, the last one—still keep the notion of validity, of a real authority for morals. These passages are not just trivial reports that the principles they mention are in fact observed; they are indignant protests that these principles are not observed. For these thinkers, standards, values and laws still have to be obeyed and respected, even though they are self-created. Nietzsche's creative individual "first maketh good and evil to be". He does not, as one might expect, make them *not* to be any longer, nor is that the message of Nietzsche's less poetic and more complex arguments in *Beyond Good and Evil*. Similarly the "revaluation of all values" that he called for was not an explosion or abolition of them all, but a new and better priority system.

The central point is always a shift in what things are called good, and in the order of preference they are set in. Though Nietzsche sometimes tried out the idea of dispensing with any moral direction whatever, all his real converting zeal was devoted to attacking existing views about what that direction should be. In explaining what the new freedom will amount to, he makes great use of polemics—refreshing blasts of fury against the fault of existing attitudes. He constantly shows that willingness to accuse others, and to explain and justify one's charges against them, which we noted earlier as marking a deliberate and serious moral judgement. For instance, in "Why I Am a Destiny" he writes:

> Have I been understood?—What defines me, what sets me apart from the rest of humanity is that I have unmasked Christian morality...The Christian has hitherto been *the* moral being... more absurd, mendacious, frivolous, harmful to himself than even the greatest despiser of mankind could have allowed himself to dream. Christian morality—the most malicious form of the will to lie, the actual Circe of mankind: that which has *ruined* it. It is *not* error as error which horrifies me at the sight of this, *not* the millennia-long lack of "good will", of discipline, of decency, of courage in spiritual affairs which betrays itself in its victory—it is the lack of nature, it is the utterly ghastly fact that *anti-nature* itself has received the highest honours as morality, and has hung over mankind as law, as categorical imperative!
>
> (Nietzsche, *Ecce Homo*, pp.131-2)

POTS AND KETTLES

How can a subjectivist philosopher be in any position to attack other people's moral views in this way? How can such a philosopher know that they are wrong? Indeed, if everyone invents their own standards, how can there be such a thing as their being wrong at all? Why, too, should readers—who are distinct people again—be interested in the views of either the attacker or the attacked? This is the paradox of this moralistic kind of subjectivism. If it keeps any recognizable moral content, it loses its sceptical standing. And again here, as we have noted often before, it is actually the moral content, not the scepticism, that gives these writings their force, their conviction and their importance.

Because Nietzsche's outgoing, serious, converting zeal was so strong, his interpreters commonly resist any attempt to classify him as a subjectivist. And on balance they are certainly right to do so. But the element of subjectivism in his writings is still very powerful, and because it was in tune with so much else in the times, it has been among the most influential of his ideas.

Sartre sees this difficulty and tries hard to meet it. In much of his writings, he preaches a straightforward and quite impressive moral message, which he explains with some vivid examples. These examples—the waiter who tells himself that his whole life is out of his control, being fixed by the role that belongs to his job; the self-styled writer who explains that it is only outside circumstances which stop him ever doing any actual writing, the young man in the war who must choose between looking after his mother and joining the Free French forces, and who hopes that somebody else can help him with this decision—all display forcibly a simple moral message: drop your excuses, do not pretend that you have no choice. Sartre is telling people to take responsibility for their own lives, because failure to do so is "bad faith". He is using the metaphysical language of existence and essence to back this precept by representing the self as unfixed, always indeterminate, capable of taking any shape, so that freedom is absolute. By accepting this description, his readers are urged to become totally free, independent, "authentic", morally self-contained.

AUTHORITY AND INDEPENDENCE

Why should these readers in their respective solitudes listen to him? Will their new independence not put them beyond his reach? After all, he is a separate person from his readers. If they listen to his impressive sermon, are they not compromising their autonomy by taking in advice from outside? Who is he to pronounce judgement that their present non-existentialist attitudes are in bad faith? Here our original question about the possibility of moral judgement comes up in a most interesting form. Sartre replies:

> We can judge, nevertheless...—and perhaps this is not a judgement of value, but it is a logical judgement—that in certain cases choice is founded upon an error, and in others upon the truth. One can judge a man by saying that he deceives himself... One may object, "But why should he not choose to deceive himself?" I reply that it is not for me to judge him morally, but I define his self-deception as an error...The attitude of strict consistency alone is that of good faith.
>
> (Jean-Paul Sartre, 1989, p. 50)

Sartre is claiming here that what we took for a moral judgement was really only a factual one. But can it be so? If we really did try to treat this judgement as merely a colourless, factual report of the offender's self-deception, there would surely be great difficulty about establishing this self-deception as a psychological fact. We would need to believe that the alleged self-deceiver is actually capable of far more freedom than he supposes; how could this be proved? To support his moral scepticism, Sartre seems to show here a very unsceptical confidence in some hazardous judgements concerning psychological facts. He takes it for granted that we can know for certain just what are the conditions under which these other people act, that we know more about them than they themselves do, and can safely convict them of deceiving themselves.

It is clear, however, that his message cannot be reduced to a merely factual judgement of this kind. The emotive, value-laden language of *good* *and bad faith* could not possibly be thus disinfected. Nor does Sartre attempt so to disinfect it. He goes on, "Furthermore, I can pronounce a moral judgement. For I declare that freedom, in respect of concrete circumstances, can have no other end and aim but itself... The actions of men of good faith have, as their ultimate significance, the quest of freedom itself as such". Freedom, then, is itself taken to be established as the supreme value—the sole value that can thus be publicly, objectively enthroned. This fairly startling value-judgement cannot be seen merely as a private memorandum addressed to Sartre by himself. It is meant to influence others, and in applying it directly to them, Sartre is quite as uninhibited, quite as accusatory as Nietzsche:

> Those who hide from this total freedom, in a guise of solemnity or with determindistic excuses, I call cowards. Others, who try to show that their existence is necessary, when it is merely an accident of the appearance of the human race on earth, I call scum.
>
> (Jean-Paul Sartre, 1989, p.52)

CAN SUBJECTIVISTS MORALIZE?

In saying that this kind of subjectivism is moralistic, I do not mean to be abusive, but simply to state an obvious fact. Both Nietzsche and Sartre have been very influential moralists, writers who have touched many people's hearts, helped them to make their decisions and affected their lives. They have altered our world. Both of them intended to do this, rather than just taking part in theoretical academic argument—an activity which Nietzsche indeed despised and rejected. Thus they were not in the long run contracting the unit of morality to a single individual. They were only trying to protect that individual from certain influences which they thought harmful. Both of them wanted the creative moral activity that they called for to have, eventually, a public application. Nietzsche seems unembarrassed about this too, writing freely (especially in the book called *Dawn or Daybreak*) of the future and the different world that he hopes to create, the world that will be produced once his message has been heard and accepted. Sartre, however, is more disturbed by the difficulty that this claim to public influence holds for subjectivism. He tries to deal with it by a strange, and apparently very demanding, doctrine of responsibility:

> Subjectivism means, on the one hand, the freedom of the individual subject and, on the other, that man cannot pass beyond human subjectivity...When we say that man chooses himself, we do mean that every one of us must choose himself; but by that we also mean that in choosing for himself he chooses for all men. For in effect, of all the actions a man may take to create himself as he wills to be, there is not one which is not creative, at the same time, of an image of man such as he believes that he ought to be...Our

responsibility is thus much greater than we had supposed, for it concerns mankind as a whole.

[The existentialist] thinks that every man, without any support or help whatever, is condemned at every instant to invent man.

(Jean-Paul Sartre, 1989, pp.52, 34)

Thus the frequent shift between "man" as an individual and as the whole species constantly tips this apparently subjectivist doctrine back into a communal application. Our free choice (it now seems) must be such that we would be happy for everybody else to take it as an example. This is an understandable notion in traditional morals—indeed, it comes from Kant. But it surely goes most oddly with Sartre's emphasis on independence, which would seem to forbid others to be influenced by our example. If each must make a private creation, nobody can take material from anybody else, and it is only by accident that any two creators might agree. This does not seem to be a way in which a public world could be shaped at all. Sartre's insistence on responsibility appears to mean that each must bear the burden of acting as he would if others were about to imitate him, although in fact they are forbidden to do this by their need for authenticity.

This tortuous position shows up a deep anomaly in what may be called moralistic or heroic subjectivism of the kind we are considering. It is an anomaly crystallised by the use of over-drastic words like "create" and "invent". Originality in morals does not need to be described in these extreme terms. It does not at all necessarily involve saying something completely new, such as "we should all keep our left eyes shut", or "the true purpose of life is the maximum production of orange-peel". Instead, it is usually a matter of suggesting a change of emphasis among existing values—a greater emphasis on independence, honesty, moral courage at the expense of other virtues—in a way that other people, too, are already beginning to suspect is necessary. (One can scarcely be said to originate something unless it manages to catch on and become available to others. But for this it is necessary that one should have a good deal in common with them.)

Of these original developments in morals the Christian exaltation of charity over vengeance is one example, the development of the ideal of tolerance after the religious wars of the 17th century is another, and the special exaltation of freedom in modern times is a third. In all these cases, no new "value" or ideal was created. New words were indeed sometimes used, and old words given rather different senses. But this does not involve the creation of new items, any more than the use of new words in the physical sciences involves the creation of new matter. What arises is a shift in attitude, in ways of thinking. The innovators have simply brought forward an existing ideal that they thought had been underemphasized and have shown good reason why it should have more attention as against other ideals, with which it had come into conflict.

The idea of creativity does have a place here, because it is very hard to have sufficient vision to see where such changes are needed and sufficient determination to make them. As in art, so in morals, we call innovators creative if they manage to produce a new and helpful positive complex by boldly rearranging existing materials. We do not insist that it shall resemble nothing earlier, nor that they shall produce it entirely out of their own heads, nor out of no materials at all. As for the idea of "inventing values" that seems much harder to use intelligibly. Invention normally means finding a new way of reaching an already agreed end. But values are supposed to be the ends themselves, the ideals towards which we direct our efforts.

EMERGENCIES AND THE BOURGEOIS PREDICAMENT

Why, then, has this exaggerated language been used? and why has it seemed so plausible and attractive? The reason surely is historical. It lies simply in the speed of change. In modern times, society has been altering so fast that unchanging habits of mind soon produce an effect of grotesque unreality. The normal need to insist on updating morals becomes drastically intensified, and it begins to seem that nothing short of a complete change will meet this need.

Here it is of considerable interest to look at the particular contexts to which these philosophers were responding. Sartre's little book *Existentialism and Humanism* is based on a lecture which he gave in 1945, and is plainly inspired by conditions during the German occupation of France during the Second World War. People who had lived contentedly for most of their lives by some fairly limited code were at this time tipped into the icy waters of an unfamiliar situation where they confronted quite different and hitherto unthinkable choices.

Sartre suggests that we see this change in rather simple terms as a contrast of illusion with reality. The humdrum, simplified bourgeois life of peacetime was not just limited, it was unreal; the chaos of wartime is real. Now this is indeed true in so far as the peacetime morality had become unrealistic, and had forgotten the surrounding parts of the world in which terrible choices were at all times going on. The self-protective pretence that all is well was indeed always an illusion. But this does not mean that the standards invoked by that peacetime morality were all baseless and its data illusory, nor indeed that the way things look in a wartime emergency cannot be deceptive too. It has not suddenly been revealed that a duty to look after one's mother or to serve one's country was always an unreal duty, simply because in a more drastic situation these two duties might conflict. Conflicts between duties are no new thing. Nor does it mean that the reasons by which we explain those duties in peacetime become unreal or irrelevant when situations get harsher.

The general background of moral thinking, which people have used for the rest of their lives, is still present in emergencies, still the backbone of their choices, even though the evils between which they are choosing become worse and the point at which their thought fails them more obvious. This continuity is very clear in the case of the young man whom Sartre describes. Why can this person not solve his difficulties by just tossing up, or by going off to Marseilles and selling nylons on the black market? In the genuinely blank situation which Sartre seems to posit these would seem to be equally possible situations, and—providing they were chosen in good faith—existentially unobjectionable: "One can choose anything, but only if it is on the plane of free commitment" he writes on page 54 of *Existentialism and Humanism*. The young man, however, holds by the standards that he always had; what he is looking for is some way of reconciling them.

Sartre talks as if the mere attempt to get advice were necessarily an evasion, an effort to make someone else take responsibility for the decision. That could of course be true, but it does not have to be. To seek advice is not the same thing as seeking as excuse. We talk with our friends in order to develop our own ideas by sharing them with others, and also to get ideas that may not have struck us yet by seeing things from their angle. We want to find out how our position looks to them, to allow the mysterious social forces that underlie all personal interaction free play to help us, to see whether things can possibly be made to look different. We want their help in getting our dilemmas into perspective, and in seeing how to accept what cannot be avoided. But in doing all this, we radically break away from Sartre's idea of a hermetically sealed individual morality. We act as social beings.

MARKS OF THE EPOCH

This brings us to a further interesting point that all these declarations from which I started have in common. They all belong essentially to our age and could probably not have been written in any other. Nietzsche, publishing in the 1880s, was among the first prophets of the sweeping individualism that we think of as typically modern, and of the elements of subjectivism that go with it. This label of modernity still confuses our view of it, because throughout the 20th century we have tended to see such notably "modern" ideas as the last word—irreversible changes. They have struck us as being scientific discoveries, as if they were disclosures forced on us by evidence which we have to accept—*facts*, perhaps scientific facts like the existence of newly-found planets or the chemical constitution of water. Nietzsche set the fashion here, and this is the point of his rhetorical remark, "God is dead". "Could it be possible?" exclaims Zarathustra. "This old saint has not yet heard in his forest that God is dead" (*Thus Spake Zarathustra*, Prologue, section 2). And this piece of cosmic news then serves as safe and central grounds for Zarathustra's sweeping rejection of all existing morality, and for the demand for the creation of totally new values.

The saint, then, is *out of date*, he is behind the times. By this Nietzsche plainly did not mean merely a matter of fashion—though unfortunately he did attach great importance to fashion and was easily seduced by the vague ideal of the Future. Nor did he just mean a failure of religion. By the death of God, he meant a set of real changes in the world, discoveries—facts—making it no longer reasonable to take into account anything outside one's own will when taking moral decisions.

What are these crucial discoveries? It is easy to name some of them. There is a new sense of the great variety of human cultures, beginning then to be established by the emerging science of anthropology. There is an equal variety revealed in past human history, along with evidence of terrible failures haunting all known moral systems. There is the complexity of human motives that began to emerge in psychological enquiries reaching from Rousseau through Freud and through much great imaginative literature, a complexity that makes it much harder to categorise people and actions as black or white. There is indeed criticism of much religious doctrine—an increasing sophistication that makes it much harder to explain morality simply as direct, divine revelation. And there is the advance of physical science, providing causal explanations for many things that had earlier been seen as direct supernatural acts.

All these are real complicating factors, undermining crude and simple views about the nature of morality. It is therefore perfectly true to say that thought on this subject today has to be more complicated than at some earlier times, simply because more data and more alternative kinds of thought are now set before us. (There have in fact been other learned epochs with this same kind of problem, for instance in China and Alexandria, but that is another story.) This increased complication, however, could scarcely mean that a sudden thunderclap has entirely changed the scene, showing irrefutably that valid moral judgement is impossible. This sweeping destructiveness is itself so incoherent and—as we shall shortly see—so incompatible with Nietzsche's own moral message that it is not a real contender for our acceptance.

Nietzsche himself, who was a poet as well as a philosopher, probably understood all this very well. He used his rhetorical exaggerations deliberately to stir up his readers' minds, driving home his new imaginative vision. The fact that he got no response at all in his own day undoubtedly made him shout the louder. But now that he, and many of his disciples, are received authorities taught in universities—something that would have appalled him—his exaggerations are taken literally as received doctrine. Hence the confident dogmatism that Allan Bloom notes in his American students today:

> There is one thing a professor can be absolutely certain of; almost every student entering the university believes, or says he believes, that truth is relative... That anyone should regard the proposition as not self-evident astonishes them, as though he were calling into question 2 + 2 = 4.
>
> (*The Closing of the American Mind*, p.25)

The fluidity of truth is seen as a discovered fact, itself a fixed truth, but also, of course, as a cherished moral certainty. Bloom goes on, "That it is a moral issue for students is revealed by the character of their response when challenged—a combination of disbelief and indignation."

This kind of uncritical conformity is clearly quite incompatible with the message of subjectivism itself, which calls on us not to go with the herd, not be intimidated by any kind of authority, and can scarcely expect us to bow to the mere prestige of a dominant fashion in our century. As we have noticed already, the odd notion of "post-modern" movements is now being used to allow present-day thought to move away from that fashion. Whether we choose to give it this name or not, such development is plainly needed. And the first form it should take naturally will be to understand fully just what the existing forms of subjectivism are supposed to be saying.

NOTES

About Nietzsche, R.J. Hollingdale's book *Nietzsche* in the Routledge Author Guides series (London, 1973) is very helpful.

Full references for quotations on pp.92-3. Quotations from some of these works also appear elsewhere in this chapter.

1. Nietzsche, *Thus Spake Zarathustra*, part 2 section 2, "In the Happy Isles"

2. Nietzsche, *Thus Spake Zarathustra*, part 3, section "Of Old and New Tables"

3. Nietzsche, *Beyond Good and Evil*, Second Article, section 43

4. Jean-Paul Sartre, *Existentialism and Humanism* (London, Methuen, 1989) p.38

5. Ibid, pp.32-33

6. Ibid, p.54

7. Ayn Rand, *The Anthem* (New York, Signet Books, New American Library, 1966) p.109

8. Ibid, p.119

9. Margaret Oldham, American psycho-therapist, interviewed in *Habits of the Heart* ed. Robert Bellah (London, Hutchinson, 1988) p.14

10. Ted Oster, ibid, p.77

Other works quoted in this chapter:

Nietzsche, *Ecce Homo*, "Why I Am a Destiny," section 7, translated by Walter Kaufmann and published with *On the Genealogy of Morals* (New York, Vintage Books, 1969).

Allan Bloom, *The Closing of the American Mind* (London, Penguin, 1987) p.25

14

The Problem of Private Validity

HAS OBLIGATION VANISHED?

One important question concerns the notion of validity or authority. Is this supposed to be still present at all, or not? Is the individual who has created values or standards then bound by them, standing under some sort of obligation to obey them? If not, the essential point of morality seems to vanish, but then in that case the whole notion of "values" seems to become meaningless too. We would not be engaged in what Nietzsche called a creation of values, or a "transvaluation of values", a change of standards. We would not be finding new directions, new and better grounds for a better set of indignations and enthusiasms. Instead we would simply be giving up, losing interest in standards altogether, dropping the whole business of pro and con, indignation and enthusiasm. Nothing would have been created.

This would be radically contrary to the spirit of both Nietzsche and Sartre, who owe the whole force of their writings to their reforming zeal, their bitter indignation against quite particular vices in contemporary society. For them plainly the authority of morals somehow remains. The individual, having generated his or her own standards, lies under an absolute obligation to live up to them. This is what Kant called "autonomy", self-rule, legislating for oneself. It has become a most important ideal in this movement of thought, but it is not altogether a clear one.

The word autonomy—self-legislation—expresses a metaphor drawn from politics. It was the word used to describe Greek colonies that had become independent of their mother-city, and the shift from this political context to a personal one, raises some puzzles. Does the past self have authority over the present one? Must we never change our principles? Or is it rather an inner centre—the true self—that rules over less central parts? What happens in cases of change, of inner conflict, or of simply becoming less interested in the matter? Most puzzling of all, how is public discussion of this kind of autonomy possible at all, and especially how can moralists be in the position to show the sharp indignation that Sartre and Nietzsche express towards people who are not autonomous enough? Is there a publicly established duty to be autonomous? But before discussing these things, it might be worth while to look again at two of the American examples that were quoted at the outset of chapter 13 to see whether they are saying something different.

At a first glance, Margaret Oldham does seem to be taking very much the same line as Sartre, and indeed it is likely that she is actually responding to Existentialist influence. There is, however, a shift. She says that loyalty to her own values is "what the universe wants from her". She plainly thinks it her business to respond to what the universe wants. Ted Oster makes an engaging attempt to get away from any such thought, but it is not clear that Mark Twain can pull this trick off for him. Mark Twain, after all, was talking in a world where people were brought up to attach a certain importance to moral standards—and so indeed was Ted Oster. In that world, we do not just discover by experiment what kinds of action leave us feeling good or feeling bad, as we might discover which foods upset our digestion. We inevitably get taught anyway what we ought and ought not to do, and alter those views as we go along. After that, what we call "feeling good" or "feeling bad" means primarily that you have done what you should or what you shouldn't. It is a matter of guilt or of a good conscience. The difference is plain when we consider that, if this really were just like a digestive matter, then somebody who felt bad after massacring helpless villagers (as at My Lai) might simply be advised to take suitable pills the next time he had occasion to do it, or to cultivate relaxation.

Fairly certainly, Ted Oster was not thinking of examples like this. But they have to be raised if what he says is to have any general interest. Oster was simply explaining how both he and Mark Twain, as individuals brought up with certain standards, found those standards operating in his emotional life. This is a question about the psychology of morals, not about morality itself. The difference can be brought out by considering that, in discussing scientific belief, one might look into the psychology of it and note how one's feeling of confidence in certain natural forces increased on grasping the laws of Newton and weakened on reading Einstein, or how one no longer felt so safe in a round world as in a flat one. However psychologically interesting these facts might be, nobody would suppose that they explained the sort of validity that belongs to scientific laws, or that physics had now somehow been "reduced" to special feelings of confidence.

THEORY AND PRACTICE

Of course these rather casual, informal remarks made during sociological interviews cannot be directly compared with the carefully expressed views of philosophers like Nietzsche and Sartre. The interviewees do not make the same pretensions, and they need a different kind of interpretation. Yet these cases are important, and important in this context, because they are practical attempts to use the very same ideas. These people are not the originators of subjectivism, but they are its disciples. They are trying to do, in their actual living, what they think the philosophers tell them to do. What is interesting is how hard they find it to be in the least consistent in doing so. The interviewers, who are sympathetic and not trying to catch them out, remark on how constantly their subjects appeal, in the details of their lives, to much more demanding and sensitive principles than they express on occasions like these, when very general principles were asked for. In practice, their morality did recognise the claims of others. But when they were asked to explain and justify that morality, the only language they seemed to possess for doing it was this thin and inadequate one, essentially egoistic and subjectivist. Even when they were asked to express their own feelings, they recited the commonplaces of contemporary individualism. But plainly they did not always live by them.

LUMPING AND SPLITTING

Plainly, the moralists who bring us nearest to subjectivism are presenting us with a genuine moral choice, a question about the kind of society that we want to live in. That question is: how cohesive shall our society be? How fully do we wish to relate, as individuals, to those around us?

Two extremes can be imagined. One would be a profoundly unified group, where the members really do not distinguish their individual interests from each others' and from the communal interests of the whole. This is the kind of situation that we may imagine to be present in an ants' or bees' nest, where the members appear to sacrifice not only their whole life's effort but also their lives quite freely for the good of the whole. The other would be a collection of enlightened egoists, each of whom really cares only about his or her own interest, and agrees only to co-operate with the others in cases shown by calculation to serve that interest.

The first pattern is of course never actually found in human life. There are smallish groups of friends, relatives or colleagues which approach much nearer to it than larger groups can. But human beings, like other social mammals and birds, evidently differ radically from the social insects in the way that their nervous systems are tuned to recognise their own individuality. The second pattern is not actually found either, but the fact that it is not has not always been so clearly acknowledged. The myth of the Social Contract is built as if that second pattern were literally true, as if we were all real "economic men". This myth—though it has had vital political uses—is not a literal statement of fact. It is, however, very powerful in our culture and is often treated as if it reported some kind of timeless truth.

The doctrine called Psychological Egoism—the belief that, as a fact, all human motives are purely self-interested—has had a lot of support from Social Contract theorists such as Hobbes. Their intention has been to save people from throwing their lives away in mistaken loyalty to rulers or churches who had no proper claim on them for this devotion. Again, the aim was a good one, but again there was overkill, excessive rhetoric, false universality. It is true that our own interests are of great importance, and that we would often do well to attend to them more than we now do. But the very fact that we are often so imprudent—the fact that we devote ourselves to all sorts of non-interested ideals, from art and warfare to mountain-climbing and motor-racing—shows plainly that our motives are not purely self-interested, but have a most complex variety of aims.

Psychological egoism is not a fact. Like many other psychological doctrines, it is a piece of propaganda. Though some degree of self-interest is indeed a part of our make-up, the question how far it shall be carried in proportion to other motives is a moral question, answered very differently in different cultures. For instance, the estimation of the claims of parents, and of elder relatives generally, is something that varies greatly. In a cross-cultural survey, people in different countries were asked to complete the sentence, "I love my mother but..." In Western countries, respondents usually saw this as a cue to make some criticism of the mother. In South-East Asia, the completion tended to be something more like, "but I can never repay all that she has done for me". It would be rather arbitrary to suggest that the Western response was somehow more authentic, nearer to basic human nature, or indeed that it was more honest than the other. It is simply a different choice, revealing a different kind of society. In recent times, the Western choice has been for more isolation, for a move to a looser, more fragmented family-system, as part of a looser, more fragmented society.

The reasons for wanting to make that choice have been fully put before us by the prophets of individualism, from Rousseau onwards through Mill and Nietzsche to Sartre and Ayn Rand, whose influential novels convey a quite extraordinary exaltation of moral solipsism—of a willingness to live as if one were the only conscious being in the universe. The rhetoric used has been intense, and the language of our age in the West is soaked in it. As I have suggested, there is much in our crowded condition of life to support this way of thinking, much to make lumping difficult and splitting attractive.

All the same, it is surely worth our while to pause and notice how certain isolating features of our life strike observers from other societies, and to ask ourselves whether this individualistic rhetoric really gives us so much moral satisfaction that we do not need to forge anything different to balance it. One such disturbing feature is indeed our treatment of the old. Another, which gradually is being corrected now but only after doing untold damage, is the inhuman isolation of small babies, brought in by pediatricians in the 1920s on very slender, supposedly "scientific" grounds, and still quite strongly persisting in a way that contrasts with the practice of most other human societies. The "medicalisation" of childbirth and the removal of the friendly female network that in most places supports women and babies through it add further strains which, I suspect, affect babies in such a way as to deepen their difficulties in dealing with others in later life.

THE NEED TO CHOOSE

People will, of course, differ greatly about how to treat this problem. The great thing is that we should be aware of it. We need to think about how best to place our society somewhere on this long spectrum of possibilities between compressing individuals into a homogeneous mass and isolating them completely; between lumping and splitting. This is typical of the choices that societies must continually make about their own formation. There are advantages and drawbacks in all sorts of positions. None of them is forced on us by human nature, and all have their price. The main thing needed in making this choice is to be aware of it, not to treat it as a foregone conclusion. (In that sense, recognition of freedom really is of the first importance—only it merely brings us to make the choice, it does not make the decision for us.) But it is important, too, to ask how this choice affects the position of moral judgement.

JUDGING NOT THAT WE BE NOT JUDGED

The wish of the splitters is to protect individuals from being subject to the judgement of others, and also from having their own judgements unduly influenced by the opinions of others. I have suggested earlier that this wish is much too sweepingly expressed, that it is not an evil to be judged by others, but only to be judged wrongly. Similarly, it is not an evil to be influenced by others, only to be influenced in wrong ways. And if we listen to what are used as anti-judgemental texts, we always find this sort of restriction built into them. Thus, what Jesus was talking about was punishment and denunciation. His message was: do not stone people, do not cast them out, do not write them off. His target was aggressive, punitive self-righteousness. His listeners were told not to regard themselves as a superior group, licensed to punish transgression. They were not told that there was no such thing as transgression ("Sin no more"). His moral spotlight was not on the original transgression at all, but on the evil response of the would-be punisher.

If we turn to Sartre, it is plain that his position too was a highly specialised one. What he had in mind was the situation of the French populace during the Second World War. *Existentialism and Humanism* expresses the bitter experience of people who had grown up with an unambitious bourgeois morality, adapted for safe and comfortable times, and who found themselves pitched into the cold and filthy water of a Nazi occupation. Many of the particular acts they had been brought up to regard as duties became impossible or irrelevant, and some of these acts would have involved helping the invaders. If they wanted to resist they might find themselves called on to rob, lie and murder. The situation in France (as opposed to, say, Norway or Poland) was peculiarly corrupting, because enough of the former establishment survived and collaborated with the Nazis to present a façade of traditional morality—to suggest that all right-thinking, *"bien-pensant"* people ought to do the same.

The peculiar disgust that this betrayal provoked accounts for Sartre's tone, and indeed it supports a depressing insight about how hollow conventional moral behaviour can sometimes be. The government and those who supported it appeared as a total sham, and since they used the habitual moral language, it seemed that decent people must move to another, completely different one. The whole tradition was stained with falsity; to find something real, one must look elsewhere. In this odious situation, the only alternatives seemed to be total revolt and total betrayal. Tradition seemed to offer no help, so individuals were called on to "invent moral values" and start again.

Yet once more the context cannot support this stark drama. Resistance was only made possible by the existence of ideals and concepts that validated it—by a long and honourable tradition of justified revolt in the cause of freedom and decency. Sartre himself stands right within that Enlightenment tradition, owing much to Descartes, Rousseau, Kant and Nietzsche. For him, as for many other people in the French Resistance, to resist was not only to fight for one's country—a quite honourable motive in itself—but to fight for the ideals conceived as having brought about the Revolution of 1789. They saw that there was no need to accept the claim of the supposed *bien-pensants* to represent the whole moral tradition. Rational, independent, rebellious morality is at least as old as Jesus and Socrates.

15

Social Darwinist Egoism

THE AMERICAN PREDICAMENT; AYN RAND

Here is a less familiar name, but ideas no less influential. Ayn Rand is a contemporary American prophet of extreme egoistic individualism. In her novels the human race appears divided into three groups. The first group, containing nearly everybody, is a mass of worthless, contented sheep known as "second-handers". They never for a moment think for themselves, and scarcely know that it would be possible to do so, but when other people do it, they respond with terrified resentment and persecute the innovators. The second group, which is tiny, contains people who do sometimes think for themselves. They are aware that the life going on around them is a senseless, unchosen existence, and they would like to introduce something better. But they cannot do this because they are not themselves original enough to provide something different. They react to this frustration either with fatalistic despair, or by perversely joining with the vulgar herd to resist and persecute the vanishingly small number of geniuses in the third group—partly from envy, partly from a sense that even this form of action is better than doing nothing. Those in the third group are terribly few, perhaps "a dozen men, down the ages". They are the genuinely creative, original people, able not only to think but to act on their own initiative. But of course, as things are, they are doomed to attract almost universal hatred, and they do the human race a service entirely against its will.

Ayn Rand's best-selling novel, *The Fountainhead*, published in 1947, is an idealised account of the architectural career of Frank Lloyd Wright. Its villains are traditional architects and their supporters, who insist on continuing their servile imitation of earlier styles and fiercely reject the modern buildings of the hero, Howard Roark. The novel is an extreme instance of the romantic cult of the lonely genius. It is also, incidentally, a splendid example of that almost religious exaltation of modernity discussed in chapter 8.

The reason for taking Ayn Rand seriously is not that she invented these ideas. Paradoxically, there is very little that is original here; the ideas are widespread and have many sources. There is surely a great deal of Nietzsche in them, notably from the crowd-hating Nietzsche represented in extract (3) at the head of chapter 13. What is interesting about Ayn Rand is that she crystallises this cluster of ideas, brings them together so determinedly and expresses them so forcefully. This fact has made her quite an influential writer. *The Fountainhead* is virtually the only book that Allan Bloom sometimes heard cited, by the American students he questioned, as having had an important influence on their lives. (In general, books mean little to them.) The book is still in print and has been frequently republished, both in the US and in Britain.

Much of *The Fountainhead* is an unremarkable social satire—sharp, often effective, and often very funny—directed against the second-handers. The peculiar thing about the book is not what it satirises but what it accepts—its naivety about the honoured groups at the top. As so often happens, a satire is betrayed by the satirist's weakness for some supposed exceptions to the general condemnation—in this case, those taken to be real individuals. The alleged strugglers after integrity are a most unconvincing bunch, and Roark himself is simply a comic-book hero, a featureless, standard he-man, a mere incarnation of virility. Much of the time, fortunately, he is strong and silent, but occasionally he makes speeches. Notably, he makes one to the jury who are trying him for dynamiting some buildings he had designed, but which other architects had inexcusably altered. Having made the expected points about artistic integrity, Roark by no means falls strongly silent, but delivers a six-page lecture on the principles of individualism. (This, rather surprisingly, persuades the jury to acquit him.) I extract a few of his sharper points, italicising some especially surprising remarks:

> *Nothing is given to man on earth.* Everything he needs has to be produced. And here man faces his basic alternative; he can survive in only one of two

ways—by the independent work of his own mind or as a parasite fed by the minds of others...

The creator's concern is the conquest of nature. The parasite's concern is the conquest of men... The basic need of the second-hander is to secure his ties with men in order to be fed. He declares that man exists in order to serve others. He preaches altruism... Men have been taught dependence as a virtue... Independence *is the only gauge of man's virtue and value.*

Men have been taught that the ego is the synonym of evil, and selflessness the ideal of virtue. But the creator is the egotist in the absolute sense, and the selfless man is the one who does not think, feel, judge or act. These are functions of the self... *All that which proceeds from man's independent ego is good. All that proceeds from man's dependence on men is evil.*

The first right on earth is the right of the ego. Man's first duty is to himself... The only good which men can do to one another and the only statement of their proper relationship is—Hands off!

Now observe the results of a society built on the principles of individualism. This, our country. *The noblest country in the history of men.* The country of greatest achievement, greatest prosperity, greatest freedom. This country was not based on selfless service, sacrifice, renunciation or any principle of altruism. It was based on a man's right to the pursuit of happiness. His own happiness. Not anyone else's. A private, personal selfish motive. *Look at the results. Look into your own conscience.*

(Ayn Rand, 1972, pp.664-70)

MORAL OR NO MORAL?

What is being said here? Once again, there is a fatal clash of aims. The ideal of a world where nobody ever listens to anybody else is at war with an irresistible desire on the writer's part to be listened to while preaching that ideal, and to shape it so that other people use their freedom in the correct way.

If the ideal of the fragmented, non-listening world prevails, we get subjectivism. In that case, each person generates and lives by a separate and wholly private morality. One of the quotations (from another novel) that I gave at the head of chapter 13 does seem to call for that approach; "Whatever road I take, the guiding star is within me; the guiding star and the lodestone which point the way". But this passage then goes on, "They point to me".

This is not only a strange and unhelpful thing for a guiding star or a lodestone to do, it is also unmistakably a piece of positive moralising. If anybody else thinks that their guiding stars and lodestones point them rather towards helping others, Ayn Rand is there to tell them that they are mistaken.

In *The Fountainhead*, this positive moralising is clearly the path chosen. There is no attempt to silence positive morality in order to avoid influencing people's individual judgements. What the book calls for is not so much independence in judgement as extreme independence in life; self-sufficiency. To call for that—especially with such passion—clearly assumes the right to influence other people's judgement. The book has a strong civic slant, it wants to change society; it is full of confident criticism both of individual lives lived in mutual, co-operative dependence and of the kind of society that is taken to be built from such lives. In fact, it is full of very sharp criticism of the vulgarity, hypocrisy and pretentiousness that the author detects in contemporary American society.

There is, therefore, something very odd and jarring about the last paragraph that I have quoted, where Roark suddenly decides to celebrate his country, not just grudgingly, as slightly less bad than others, but quite uncritically, in the spirit of a flag-waving presidential candidate.

BELIEVING IN THE SURVIVAL OF THE FITTEST

What has come crashing in here is Social Darwinism—the extra element that distinguishes most English-speaking individualism today sharply from its continental forerunners. The myth that glorifies commercial freedom by viewing it as part of a huge, self-justifying cosmic evolutionary process, and exalts it as the model for all social life, was brought to America by Herbert Spencer in the 1880s. It has little to do with Darwin, and nothing at all to do with serious biology. It has always been centrally a metaphysical way of justifying economic policies, using some selected biological stories as its persuasive myth. Spencer was its main progenitor, though it has sources further back, such as Adam Smith. But Spencer, being extremely ignorant of biology, mistakenly supposed that he could support it from Darwin's biological theories, and the idea has stuck. This quasi-evolutionary view had such a success in the United States that for a long time Spencer's work outsold, in that country, those of every other philosopher.

It is essentially a public and political myth, confidently recommending a particular way of running society. This means that the kind of individualism associated with it is quite different from Nietzsche's kind, which was anarchic, antipolitical and disillusioned with all institutions. It is equally different from Sartre's, which existed to provide a channel for alienation from one particular existing system. After the war, Sartre was always looking for better systems, and was for a long time drawn to Marxism. But he continued to see a great deal of difficulty in bringing his individualism to terms with any political forms. Ayn Rand, by contrast, seems in passages like these to see no difficulty at all in fitting her (officially very demanding) ideas of personal freedom into the framework of that very corporate thing, modern Western-style plutocracy. And there are many other people in the West today who don't seem to find this difficult either.

THE ELUSIVENESS OF SUBJECTIVISM

All that needs to be said about this remarkable feat from our present angle is that it shows, once more, how what looked like a sweeping sceptical position about the whole of morality turns out to be just one more moral position. Once again, an apparent case of subjectivism proper, in the sense of a real programme of separating the thoughts of every moral agent from every other, is really something much more modest philosophically—though still startling enough considered as a moral position.

On this more modest ground, subjectivism is often useful. There is indeed often a point in directing attention to the subjective *aspect* of morals—to the inner life, to personal choice, to the way people feel about what they do and what they believe. All the prophets mentioned here say some excellent things to that effect, and if one means by subjectivism only that, there is a lot to be said for it. But it is not a way of avoiding moral judgement.

HEROIC OR THERAPEUTIC ISOLATION?

Before leaving this topic, it seems necessary to say something about the interesting question of tone. The quotations I have used in the chapter have mostly celebrated individualism in a style that is moralistic, heroic and somewhat aggressive—as a clarion-call to individuals to stand up bravely and fight against an oppressive society. The model is Ajax defying the lightning. But there exists also today what may be called therapeutic individualism—a rather plaintive request to be left alone by society, on the ground that one is not really feeling very well.

This request seems to have a fairly direct connection with the campaign for universal detachment, which we have just been considering. Here again, the development is most noticeable in America, but seems to belong to a set of ideals, viewed as modern, that are far more widely pursued.

Worries about mental health became prevalent in the United States towards the end of the 19th century. Freud, when he went there in 1909, aroused great interest, but the questions he raised were already under discussion there. Already, before his visit, "some ninety medical articles on 'psychotherapy' had been published there, and the term had been designated a separate topic in the official medical index" (Robert Bellah, 1988, p.121).

Sources of the trouble are not too hard to find:

> As nineteenth-century Americans came increasingly to see, life on the escalator was anything but easy. Just when he could count on fewer and fewer people for "unconditional acceptance," the individual had to be self-disciplined, competitive, ambitious, able to respond to rapidly changing situations and demands... It was under these conditions that a concern for mental health became a central American preoccupation, and a wide variety of therapeutic nostrums appeared... What most of the forms consist in (today) is a relationship between a patient (or client) and a professional therapist.
>
> (*Habits of the Heart*, p.120)

The authors point out that this therapeutic seclusion is a rather unusual arrangement. As another study puts it:

> Psycho-analysis (and psychiatry) is the only form of psychic healing that attempts to cure people by detaching them from society and relationships...

All other forms (shamanism, faith-healing, prayer) bring the community into the healing process. Modern psychiatry isolates the troubled individual from the currents of emotional interdependence and deals with the trouble by distancing from it and manipulating it through intellectual/verbal discussion, interpretation and analysis.

This strategy is not accidental, but goes with a distinctive moral approach, in which special protection is held to be necessary while the self is under reconstruction. It is held that:

The individual must find and assert his or her true self because this self is the only source of genuine relationships to other people. External obligations, whether they come from religion, parents or social conventions, can only interfere with the capacity for love and relationships.

For instance

A counsellor who runs a therapy group for divorced women tries to help them feel more independent... When pressed to consider obligation in relationships, she answers, "I guess, if there is anyone who needs to owe anybody anything, it is honesty in letting each other know how they feel about each other, and that if feelings change, to be open and receptive to accept these changes, knowing that people in relationships are not cement".

(Veroff, Kulka and Douvan, 1981, p.101)

Here, surely, we have once more a wildly exaggerated statement of a quite modest moral point. It is very natural for a counsellor who is occupied in helping the divorced to deal with unreal feelings of guilt to get reductive and dismissive about obligation. But if nobody had—literally—ever recognised that they owed anybody any obligation apart from the honesty needed to tell them when they no longer loved them, most of us would be dead. Our parents gave us the tiresome and exhausting care that we needed in infancy, sometimes no doubt because they felt like it, but at other times because they knew that they owed it to us, and responded to the obligation. Human life would be impossible if this sort of recognition did not continually fill the gaps that inevitably appear in our natural helpful motivations.

JUST A MATTER OF PRIORITY?

Therapeutic language does not, of course, normally treat the seclusion it recommends as intended to be permanent. It points the patient forward to a time when outer relations can be taken up again—indeed, when they will become much better and more rewarding—but it warns that this cannot happen until justice has first been done to the self. Inner cleanliness, inner freedom, inner autonomy come first:

> Thus the therapeutic ideal posits an individual who is able to be the source of his own standards, to love himself before he asks for love from others, and to rely on his own judgement before deferring to others. Needing others in order to feel "O.K." about oneself is [seen as] a fundamental malady that therapy seeks to cure.

> (*Habits of the Heart*, p.99)

IS ANYBODY WELL?

Again, this is understandable as a piece of crisis-management for particular cases—for abnormal dependence, abnormal submissiveness and conformity. Or again, it can be seen as a half-truth of value for all of us. Self-respect, self-understanding, and indeed self-love, are necessary parts of serious living; they are not guilty excesses; we vitally need them. As Bishop Butler put it in his Preface to the Sermons (1726), "The thing to be lamented is, not that men have so great regard to their own good or interest in the present world, *for they have not enough,* but that they have so little to the good of others". Our own inner welfare is indeed a prime concern for each of us, and we do sometimes need to withdraw from others in order to attend to it.

But it is surely alarming to preach this gospel as normal and comprehensive advice for most people. Indeed, there is something strange about the whole situation in which it is normal for most people, if not for everybody, to be considered as ill enough to need this special treatment. There seems, too, to be something strange and ambiguous about the exceptional position of the therapist in this kind of world. He or she is apparently the only person who may legitimately be depended upon. For the duration of the treatment, clients or patients must depend deeply on their therapists. There are, moreover, some styles of therapy that do not even expect a cure, but treat this dependent relationship as a permanent one.

If one removes this rather extreme element, the therapeutic ethic emerges as mainly a matter of priorities. It says that each of us will not be able to relate properly to our neighbours until we have sorted out our own inner problems. This is often sound advice. But is it any sounder than the corresponding half-truth, which Bernard Shaw once wrote in a letter to Wells—"We must reform society before we can reform ourselves...personal righteousness is impossible in an unrighteous environment"? The truth seems to be that both things have to go on together.

NOTES

Works quoted in this chapter:

Ayn Rand, *The Fountainhead* (Glasgow, Collins, 1972) pp.664-70

Robert Bellah, ed., *Habits of the Heart* (London, Hutchinson, 1988) pp.99, 120, 121)

Veroff, Kulka and Douvan, *Mental Health in America* (New York, Basic Books, 1981) pp.6-7, 101

Bishop Butler, Preface to the Sermons (1726), section 40; (see also Sermons 11 and 12)

16

Moving Forward Through the Modern World

WHAT WE CAN STILL SEE

So far, then, the morally impressive campaigns against "moral judgement" have always proved to be one-sided, aimed not against judgement itself, but against particular ill-judgers. Do we now want to enlarge our scope and launch a different kind of campaign? Do we now have reason to say that, under present conditions, not only is it wrong to accept the judgements made by a corrupt and cowardly society, but it is equally wrong to accept any judgements made by anybody, and further—a different point—that it is wrong to make such judgements ourselves?

If we do want to say this, the reason would presumably be something to do with the increased complexity of modern life—with a sense that the problems have now simply become too large for us. It is certainly true that we ought to recognise this complexity, that we should not confidently claim to legislate finally for all times and all observers, as people have sometimes done in the past. But—boring as it may be to mention it—this is yet again one moral judgement, recommending modesty and diffidence. The situation is not that we cannot see what is happening at all, simply that we are increasingly aware that we might make mistakes. But that is true on factual questions too, yet we know that we must sometimes decide those.

When we have to decide—today—who to vote for, or what to give to a charity, or whether to have a row with our friends, we have to decide this as the people we are, in our present circumstances. The fact that 12th-century Sicilians or present-day Solomon Islanders, or even people like us in ten years' time, might have reason to view the decision differently does not affect what we should think today. (We will look further at this problem of possible hypothetical refuters in the next chapter.)

Giving up judging is certainly not the only option that remains to us. In fact, though our present predicament is confusing, it is not so much more confusing than that of many people in the past as is often suggested. Once the point where individuals lose their bearings is reached, further additions to the general confusion do not necessarily make much difference. One can drown just as well in seven feet of water as in seventy. And even if the present situation were exceptionally confusing, it is not clear that that would be a reason to stop trying to understand it. People in very complex situations need not lose their moral bearings altogether, just as they can keep their sense of up and down in all but the most violent physical upsets.

We can see how this unnoticed background of familiar values is still taken for granted, even in very unfamiliar circumstances, if we think about the situation of Sartre's student, wondering whether to join the Free French army or stay to look after his mother. This man's position was certainly very confusing, at least as complex as many of ours. Yet he knew enough about his moral situation to rule out all courses except two, although there must have been many other tempting ones that would have saved him from that dilemma. He still had large, well-founded background judgements about matters like the Nazi ethic, which narrowed down his possible courses enormously. And that is evidently still true of ourselves. If we start to imagine what it would be like to be cut off by the complications of the modern world from all possible moral comment whatever—to be quite uncertain whether to approve or disapprove of the most despotic and oppressive governments and their torturers, and of the most iniquitous private behaviour—it is hard to see what such a condition would be like. It is not obvious what moral reasons could call on us to deprive ourselves of our power of judgement in this general and drastic way.

PROCESSES OF FRAGMENTATION

Are there reasons of other kinds? Some possible ones arising from the nature of knowledge will confront us again in the next chapter. But if we ask for psychological reasons—for considerations which are inclining people in general to move in this direction—it seems important to bear in mind that this tendency may simply be part of a general retreat from each other of individuals in modern society, a more or less deliberate self-protective policy of drifting apart. This policy no doubt has some moral advantages, and certainly has strong natural causes in the painful pressures of our crowded lives. To some extent, it may be a necessary movement. But it has already gone very far, and its further development surely needs to be more sharply recognised and questioned.

Besides the difficulties already mentioned, there are, as we have just seen, reasons for concern about this movement on the grounds of mental health. In the last few decades, psychiatrists and therapists have been reporting, not only an increase in what is generally classed as mental illness, but also a shift from the kinds of neuroses involving diseased relations with other people—the kind that chiefly occupied Freud—to other kinds, notably depression, which isolate people and make it hard for them to relate to anyone else at all, however unsatisfactorily. It also seems of some interest that, in the USA—the most individualistic of communities, and also the most "modern" in other ways—recourse to psychiatrists and therapists is increasingly a much more accepted, normal thing than it is in Europe. This is not, of course, to say that people are any crazier, but to note a difference in the way in which their difficulties can be viewed.

EFFECTS ON POLITICS

As has been suggested in chapter 8, there seems to be something about the individualistic approach that makes it more natural to deal with social friction by looking inward and trying to adjust the individual rather than by looking outward and trying to change the institutions. In this way, political means of reform can be forgotten, and if all citizens regard themselves as morally isolated, this is likely to happen. Though each of us may feel some pressure from bad institutions, it does not happen very often that pure calculations of self-interest alone will make it seem worthwhile for individuals to throw themselves into the work of political reform. Thus it can turn out—paradoxically—that the Enlightenment's insistence on the priority of the individual over society can prove self-defeating.

The contributors to *Habits of the Heart* view this problem as central—speaking of the USA but thereby, as I have suggested, of every society that views itself as "modern", Robert Bellah comments:

> The tension between self-reliant competitive enterprise and a sense of public solidarity espoused by civic republicans has been the most important unresolved problem in American history... As we unthinkingly use the oxymoron "private citizen", the very meaning of citizenship escapes us. And with Ronald Reagan's assertion that "we the people" are a "special interest group", our concern for the economy being the only thing that holds us together, we have reached a kind of end of the line. The citizen has been swallowed up in "economic man".

(Robert Bellah, 1988, pp.256 and 271)

Yet this kind of economic liberalism is not ultimately liberating...

NOTES

Works quoted in this chapter:

Robert Bellah, ed., Habits of the Heart (London, Hutchinson, 1988) pp.256, 271.

17

Doubts, Reasonable and Otherwise

PROBLEMS ABOUT CERTAINTY

We come back now to issues about the nature of knowledge—to the question whether moral judgement is in some sense impossible because we do not have knowledge about values.

Throughout the central part of this book, we have been occupied with moral questions, because many of the reasons that have led people to reject the possibility of moral judgement have proved to be moral reasons. These reasons spring from objections to a particular set of bad judgements, or to bad conduct associated with those judgements. They are not epistemological, not attacks on the possibility of knowledge about morals. But that quite different kind of attack does also exist and, because of the prestige of knowledge today, even people who would not normally be drawn to such subjects need to think about it.

There are real problems about the limits of knowledge. What is it to know something for certain?

As we have seen, the founders of modern science in the 17th century faced this question, because they were trying to put knowledge of the physical world on a sounder footing than it had ever occupied before. Descartes, the philosopher who came forward with an answer, was especially concerned to get a proper basis for this work—in particular, for the physics of Galileo and the mechanistic biology of William Harvey (notably the circulation of the blood). It was hoped that developments of this kind would eventually make it possible to display the physical world completely as a vast, fully knowable and predictable deterministic machine, comparable with the good clockwork which was then beginning to astonish the learned world.

This simple mechanistic model served science well until quite late in the 19th century. But it is worth our while to notice at once that, since that time, its ambitions have been shown to be much higher than is either reasonable or necessary. Physics, diving further and further into the structure of matter, has not found a single great intelligible clock. It has found instead various usable islands of partial order in a larger, "chaotic" background that may well be in principle impenetrable to our reason. On current views, the prospect is not just that we will take a long time to discover some final "secret of the universe", which will make everything predictable, but that we could not possibly do so, since many things are not predictable at all, even in principle.

DESCARTES' EXPERIMENT

It is not in the least surprising, however, that 17th-century observers hoped to do better than this, and looked for a scientific methodology that would provide final and absolute certainty. To supply a proper basis for this sort of science, Descartes made two dramatic and impressive demands. First, there had to be a single, absolutely secure starting-point from which everything else would follow, and then a logically impregnable set of connections fixing all other truths securely to that starting-point. Himself a great mathematician, Descartes pictured the resulting structure of thought on the model of a gigantic mathematical system with a single axiom.

To find this axiom, he doubted, and advised his readers to doubt, systematically, everything they had previously thought they knew. When he had poured this acid over the whole mental scene, Descartes reported that only one thing still remained undissolved—namely, his own consciousness, his knowledge that he himself was there thinking. Everything outside him he could doubt, but not that. If he tried to doubt it, he himself would necessarily still be there as a doubting subject. "I think; therefore I am".

In his use of this single solid starting-point Descartes compared himself with Archimedes, who—on discovering the principle of the lever—said that if he had a suitable place to put his lever, he could shift the whole earth. Using this one premiss or sky-hook as his foundation, Descartes went on to prove—by highly formal arguments that need not now concern us—the existence of a good God. From that he argued that, since a good God is not a deceiver, our faculties are not deceptive, and can, if carefully and systematically employed, be relied on to give us the truth about the world.

Though the sky-hook approach would not be popular today, Descartes' insistence on method, on the importance of careful and systematic connections of thought, did prove vital for the development of modern science. In particular, his stress on the use of mathematics was vital for physics. It was not surprising, then, that the notion of aiming at absolute intellectual security, and providing it by logical moorings to an unshakable foundation, commanded great respect. It so happened, too, that Descartes' choice of human consciousness to provide that point accorded well with the increasing interest in individual psychology during the centuries that followed. Because of his radical attempt to go back to the beginning, his *Discourse on Method* and his *Meditations* remain among the most exciting and most useful of philosophical books.

DOUBT NEEDS DIRECTION

But, along with the methodical science that he launched, the enquiries that Descartes started about the nature of knowledge were vigorously pursued too, and they soon raised difficulties about the model he had chosen—the metaphor of *building on foundations*. He had done his original destructive work only too well. The trouble about systematic doubt is that, once started, it does not stop at the point he had scheduled for it. Indeed, it cannot easily be stopped at all. It is a solvent that finally leaves no foundation to build on.

IRRATIONAL DOUBTING

If we set ourselves on principle to attack every proposition in sight, not just by asking whether, in our present circumstances, we have already some reason to doubt it, but by asking whether there could be any such reasons in any circumstances whatever, we can almost always imagine such a reason. Even if we do not see it at once, we can still suspect that we are not being imaginative enough. We might, for instance, be dreaming. Even about

simple arithmetic we can, after all, make mistakes. Besides, even if we are
not now making any, might there not be some new, post-Einsteinian kind
of arithmetic which we cannot now begin to imagine, by which two and
two would not equal four after all?

We certainly do constantly make mistakes about the reasoning that
connects our various beliefs together. And certainly Descartes' cherished
starting-point, "I think", begins to look much less solid once you start to
ask awkward questions about its meaning. *What* am I? Am I just an
instantaneous thought? Am I a dreamer? or do I really have the past that
my fallible memory seems to report? This kind of query proved a grave
worry, leading into wider problems about personal identity. In general, it
gradually emerged that undirected, undiscriminating doubt is not a much
better guide than undirected, undiscriminating belief. What matters is not
really whether you make a habit of believing or disbelieving, but whether
you are in control of your habits, and on what principles you direct them.
In fact, general, arbitrary doubt cannot really be called systematic, it is
rather compulsive or obsessive. This point is fully argued in Ludwig
Wittgenstein's little book *On Certainty.*

More far-reaching systematic doubt thus brought on a much more
general destructive scepticism—not just about outlying matters, nor about
value-judgements, but about the whole of knowledge. The over-ambitious
search for perfectly secure knowledge ended, as over-ambitious projects
often do, in a paralysing disillusion, not just by chance, but because this
was its logical terminus. David Hume was the classical prophet of this
sweeping, all-purpose scepticism. The science-oriented tradition of
Descartes has never managed to expel this enemy within. If we want to
avoid its pathless swamps and to put it in proportion, a quite different
approach is needed.

FACTS AND VALUES

However this logical difficulty about Descartes' position was not much
noticed for a time except by philosophers. The view accepted by scientists
and the general public has drifted instead towards the quite narrow,
one-sided purpose for which it was first designed—towards simply vali-
dating physical science and mathematics. As we saw in chapter 3, this view
has largely ignored the vast range of other propositions that we all accept,

and must accept if human life (including science) is to go on at all. This one-sided view has taken form in a single crude division between "facts" and "values"—facts being deemed to be knowable and (somewhat arbitrarily) confined to science; values not being thought knowable because they were held not to involve propositions at all but merely feelings. Values were then, in the common language mentioned earlier, "just a matter of your own subjective point of view" or "a matter of opinion".

It has by now grown plain that this is an unworkable system. Its confusions have been becoming more disturbing all through the 20th century, when the profound and incoherent scepticism about values that was always implicit in it has been gradually drawn out and expressed. By "scepticism" is meant here—as suggested earlier—not a healthy readiness to ask questions and try to answer them, but an arbitrary, undiscriminating habit of denying that anything can be known on the whole subject, an unwillingness to think—an advance rejection of all answers, which in fact is not compatible with the serious asking of any questions at all.

TROUBLE WITH STANDARDS

This weird position has seemed necessary because of an artificial heightening of the standards of knowledge. As with any other kind of standard, very narrow and demanding notions of knowledge simply have the effect of artificially narrowing the scope of what is said to be known. Like other deliberately raised standards, they do not necessarily improve what is available; they may just make people describe it differently. If the seal of approval is given only to products better than any that can possibly be made, users reasonably lose interest in seals of approval. And again, if the seal of approval is conferred for something irrelevant—say, in the case of cars, for a specially elegant design of the underside—it becomes necessary to find a different set of standards for evaluating the things that we actually have to choose.

This is why there seems little point in the sweeping, undiscriminating scepticism recommended by Hume and Unger. "Standards" are not things that exist as ends in themselves, things whose value could be increased by continually raising them. Standards have a function; they exist to make it possible to discriminate between the better and worse among the things that are available. There is only a point in raising standards when this will make possible real improvements in the things that they measure.

At the Renaissance this did of course really happen with scientific standards. By insisting that more certainty could be reached, and by showing how to reach it, the scientists and philosophers of that time showed the possibility of modern science and launched it on its path. And this was a tremendous achievement.

Yet the first move in this game—the raising of the standard of certainty—only had a point in so far as it made the next move possible. It was a means to that end, not an act laudable in itself. Once this had been done, continued standard-raising has no obvious point, and—when it is not done for the moral reasons we have discussed earlier—it begins to look like a mere idle, obsessive habit. There is no point in concentrating further on polishing up the concept of knowledge. It is better to turn to other parts of the conceptual scene, where real difficulties are arising.

That is why English-speaking philosophers have very largely dropped the intense interest that they long displayed in the nature of knowledge. But the public has not so far followed their example. Because of the immense prestige of science, the apparent dilemma for concepts seeking to be thought respectable remains. These concepts had better look knowable—indeed in some sense scientific—or they may be suspected of being absolute nonsense.

EMOTIVISM

Officially, this alarming fate was not supposed to happen to ideas about value. The people who have excluded morality from knowledge have usually explained politely that they did not mean to downgrade its importance by doing so; they were merely reclassifying it in a neutral way. If anything, the segregation of values from facts was supposed to make the notion of knowledge itself become less weighty—the compliment paid by that word less necessary. Judgements about values would then not lose their importance, they were only being reclassified as feelings rather than as pieces of knowledge.

This was the doctrine called logical positivism. Attempts to take the sting out of its effect on values by treating it as a mere reclassification could not really work, because their reclassification was made against a background where, in real life, the distinction between mere unreflective feeling and serious judgement still remained and kept its enormous practical importance. Everybody takes a thoughtful, well-defended moral position more seriously than a purely impulsive one. That difference could not be made to vanish simply by a shift in the boundaries on knowledge. Nor did most of those who stressed the fact-value gap even want to make it vanish.

When they thought of value-judgements some of them—notably A.J. Ayer—seem to have had in mind a set of conventional moral judgements of which they disapproved in any case, and which therefore they did not at all mind downgrading. Others—notably Hume—were fairly conventional in their own morality, and took it for granted that the feelings of others would agree with their own, provided that certain simple mistakes were avoided. They therefore believed that spontaneous moral agreement could be secured simply by natural harmony of feeling without the need for serious argument. And it is, of course, exactly in cases of conflict that the real need for moral thinking arises.

THE IMPORTANCE OF DEGREES

It is time to pick up here some of the thoughts about the nature of knowledge mentioned in chapter 3. Just what claims are we making when we say we know something?

The concept of knowledge is not a simple on-off affair. Knowledge of any kind is not a solid possession that you have or do not have, like a house. Knowledge has degrees, we can know things more or less well or thoroughly.

Knowledge is a facility, a capacity, a skill. To say "I know this" is not just to say, "I have got this proposition down in my memory, or in the memory of my computer". As we all know—and it is worth noticing that we have a right to say we know it—memories can contain propositions that we do not understand at all. If, however, we claim to know them, we mean something more like, "I am in control of this set of thoughts; I understand them, I can manage them". If someone wants to cast doubts on whether we really do know what we claim to know, their proper response is not to ask for our proof of legal title to the property. It is certainly not to say, "How do you know that you know it?"—a question that is sometimes brought into these discussions, but whose meaning is quite obscure and which it is hard to think of an occasion for asking. The doubter's proper response is to say, "Go on then; use these concepts, Show me how you *do* it".

THE PROBLEM OF THE HYPOTHETICAL REFUTER

What difference should it make to our knowledge-claims if we think it possible that somebody, in some different situation, might be in a position to deny what we now think we know? This possibility is much more real to us today than it has been to most people in earlier times. That is why it is not yet fully built in to the traditional concept of knowledge. We may need to reshape that concept slightly to allow for it.

The best way of doing this surely is to assume that normally our claims to knowledge are understood to carry an implicit health warning, saying something to the effect that we do not claim to be infallible and have not searched the whole range of possibilities to find out whether somebody else will one day correct us. More simply, we could just say that we no longer give the guarantee that perhaps used to be expected, which said that we, as knowers, were infallible to the end of time. Guarantees of infallibility are, as the Catholic Church has found, awkward things, and sensible people do not usually expect to get them with the intellectual goods they buy.

It is not clear, however, that there ever really was such a guarantee. The position is probably rather that people used not to raise such a question at all. Because the answer is obvious once you do raise it, the health warning does not need to be spelt out. Nobody would be fool enough to doubt it. It is understood that what we mean if we claim to know something now is that we have applied the standards of certainty that are now normally thought appropriate for such suggestions, and that, as far as we can see, this one is all right. That much we do guarantee. Beyond that, nobody can go.

Newton, when he proclaimed his laws of motion, was not asked about Einstein. Somebody might well have asked him whether he was sure that his laws were true and complete. This might have been just a friendly enquiry about the amount of confidence he felt, in which case the answer would plainly have been a matter of degree. Or, more interestingly, it might have been an enquiry about the degree of confidence he thought he *ought* to feel—the standards he thought should be applied. It is very likely that, in this case, he would have given some quite complex answer about the various standards that might be relevant. He did say, "I do not make hypotheses"—meaning, apparently, that he did not make mere loose speculations or guesses. He intended, then, to state with some confidence what was the case. And he committed himself fully to the propositions he put forth as doing this. But this is a different thing from claiming to be infallible.

THE NEED FOR COMMITMENT

Commitment of this kind is necessary for effective discourse, because if everybody holds back from endorsing everything they say, no speech is reliable and we lose the advantage of speaking at all. (Someone who kept adding, "Of course this may not be true", to every sentence would simply be a public nuisance.) Words like "certain" and "know" and indeed "truth" are part of this language of commitment. Perhaps the strongest form of commitment is to say something like, "I am as sure of this as I am of anything", and this Newton could quite reasonably have done. Beyond that he could not go. Neither could Einstein, nor can his successors today, nor will anybody ever be able to.

NOTES

Hume's wholesale scepticism may be most easily studied in his *Treatise of Human Nature* Book 1 Part Four, "Of the Sceptical and Other Systems of Philosophy". Its meaning is far from clear. In part, it is simply a matter of combining various particular destructive arguments which he had used in other contexts to attack particular widely-held positions. But even destructive arguments always involve some positive beliefs, and all these arguments have other important points to make besides their destructive ones—points which could in their turn be attacked and destroyed. The notion of a universal destructiveness giving a sense to all the destruction is extremely mysterious. Hume sometimes suggests that his scepticism will make no difference to life, which suggests that it is merely a mild general caution against over-confidence. Yet he plainly attached far more importance to it than this could involve, and thought it far more frightening.

In modern times, Humian scepticism has been revived and developed by Peter Unger in *Ignorance* (Oxford University Press, 1975) and other writings.

About Facts and Values, Geoffrey Warnock's little book *Contemporary Moral Philosophy*, (London, MacMillan, 1967) describes very clearly how this distinction arose and what went wrong with it. On how to put it right, Julius Kovesi's *Moral Notions* (London, Routledge, 1967) is unbeatable. See also various papers in my *Heart and Mind, the Varieties of Moral Experience* (London, Methuen Paperback, 1983) notably "Is 'Moral' a Dirty Word?".

Emotivism. This too stems from Hume, especially from *A Treatise of Human Nature*, Book III, Part 1, Sections 1 and 2. Its real popularity has, however, stemmed largely from A.J. Ayer's *Language, Truth and Logic* (London, Gollancz, 1936). Ayer gave Hume's doctrine a modern linguistic dress, arguing that language could only have meaning when it described sense experience, so that value-judgements, which did not describe it, were strictly "nonsense", speech without meaning, designed merely to express emotion or to produce it in others. (This is "logical positivism".) The book made a considerable stir and has been one of the few philosophy-books written in English in this century to be widely read. Its author, who was only twenty-six when he wrote it, has had to spend much of his later life unsaying what he said then, because when looked at seriously it does not make a lot of sense. The study of language has not supported Logical Positivism. It turns out that not much of intelligible language is in fact used to describe sense-experience. Meaningfulness does not usually depend on subject matter so much as on context and connection, and the expression of emotion is not meaningless, but can be a fully structured and articulate form of sense.

Logical Positivism, however, had a wide influence, because the offer to exempt speech on moral subjects from the normal standards of sensible discourse found a lot of takers. It was welcome, not only to people like Ayer who did not want to discuss these things, but also to others who did, and who found it very hard to do so intelligibly. It found an echo, too, in the traditional idea that certain very sacred things are indeed unintelligible and inexpressible. It is an exaggeration of some important half-truths about the difficulties of communication.

18

What About Values?

CALL IN THE CONTEXT

Factual statements, then, do not carry a guarantee of completeness and finality. When we understand this, we have largely got rid of the false contrast between an absolute and infallible kind of factual knowledge and a supposedly loose speculation about values. The question about value-judgements then gets much easier.

The two kinds of case are actually much more alike than is often suggested. Both about facts and values, we know that opinions do vary and do change. We know therefore, if we think about it, that our own views—on both topics equally—are not the complete and final truth, not the last word. If we are in doubt about propositions of either kind, we do not—in either case—look for a foundation-type justification that rests on a single premiss, itself hanging unsupported in space. Instead we use, both for facts and values, a network of explanations linking the point we want to question with others that have their own kind of evidence, and relating it to the whole map of our experience, and of the world which we believe to surround us.

If we are considering getting rid of an opinion of either kind, what we need to do is to see how much else would have to go if we lose it, and how much will have to go if we keep it. For instance, supposing that there is really no particular objection to murdering anyone whom one wants out of the way, as the character I quoted from P.D. James in chapter 1 suggested, how will this affect the rest of life? How will we then view those around us, if we think them disposable at will, and presumably expect them to think the same about us? Such changes are not isolated.

As the Macbeths found, they cannot be kept in watertight compartments, they often spill over to transform life completely. Even much smaller changes than this can have wide and unexpected effects. For instance, the process of emancipating oneself from quite small demands of conventional custom can transform life for better or worse—a point which many novelists have explored.

What supports value-judgements, then, is not some invented logical premiss, but their relation to the whole of life—a whole that these judgements are continually being used to criticise and change. This whole is not, of course, confined to each single person's experience, nor to one society. It extends to the boundary of their information. In fact this wide connectedness is the source of a difficulty that non-argumentative people often feel if asked to give a single reason for an accepted moral judgement, to explain why (for instance) it is wrong to murder people. There are a thousand reasons for murder being wrong, and it is not easy for the person questioned to know where to start on them unless some special reason emerges why the question is being asked—unless, for instance, there is a known wish to justify some particular murder.

When the moral judgements of a society do change—for instance, when people turn against cruel punishments, or begin to think that they ought to show some consideration for animals—this does not happen suddenly and alone. It is part of a wider change of attitudes, affecting parts of life not thought of as particularly moral matters at all—the kind of sympathies and revulsions that are felt, the customs that come naturally, the games that are played. But because this change is sweeping, for it to happen at all, there must be seeds growing in the culture for a long time, producing at first mainly uneasiness, conflict and distress. Even small moral changes are not easy and large ones are desperately hard; they go with total transformation of life.

By contrast, at times large changes in factual beliefs can be quite rapid and make little immediate difference to the social scene. Newton's laws could be proclaimed without a political revolution. Galileo did indeed get into trouble for supporting Copernicus, but that seems to have been due much more to a local political storm than to any necessity for conflict over the views themselves, which were in general reasonably held to be too remote from ordinary life to be worth fighting about. It is quite true that, as time went on, Newton's and Copernicus' views were gradually woven into a new imaginative world-picture which did affect life, and the same thing is now happening with their successors. But if one asks: which kind of belief is the more secure? Is it the accepted laws of physics or the basic moral laws of society? the answer would surely have to be the moral laws. They are woven into everything we do, and cannot be changed without bringing society itself to a standstill. And, as two scientific revolutions have shown us, this is not true of physics.

WHAT SECURITY DO WE NEED?

In both cases, security means interwovenness, a relatively central position in the web of experience. It cannot be absolute, nor is it clear what is being demanded if we think that it should be. It is surely a presupposition of normal thought that the world is larger than we know, and contains things—both moral and physical—unheard of by us, things not dreamt of in our philosophy. This sense of vastness does not really conflict with our other presupposition that we must take seriously the things that we do manage to dream of, and commit ourselves honestly to the part of the truth that we have so far managed to see. ("Truth" is of course another word that has been distorted and made to look unattainable in the same way as "knowledge", which is why some people have helpfully suggested that there is no such thing as truth. For it, too, that pressure should be resisted. The word "truth" stands primarily for "the right answer". And to ask questions of any kind is to commit oneself to the view that there is such an answer.)

There is certainly often tension between the presupposition of vastness and the need for commitment, and often great difficulty in doing justice to both. Both, however, seem so obviously necessary that it is not really plausible to try and resolve this trouble by getting rid of one of them. This whole difficulty, and the presence of constant disagreement that makes it obvious, should not, I think, surprise us too much in a species that nobody supposes to be perfect, and it certainly should not lead us to talk as if all opinions have been shown to be equally groundless.

There are two ways in which we can make the occurrence of disagreement more intelligible. There is first the general fact that the truth is vast; nobody can be expected to have all of it. Second, there are many particular facts that explain divergence. Equally about facts and values, the different opinions held in different times and places belong to people living differently, confronting different options and using different kinds of evidence. Relativists are right to stress the difference this makes, and to claim that sometimes we can use it to resolve disagreement.

THE MEANING OF MORAL DIVERSITY

An instance of this understandable variation on the factual side is Newton's case, just now discussed. An instance on the moral side is the traditional Inuit (Eskimo) practice of leaving old people ceremonially to die in a specially built hut when their relatives could no longer support them. This was one of a range of practices forced on people living at subsistence level, because it was simply impossible to keep everyone alive, and some sort of choice had to be made about who should go first. No doubt before resorting to it these peoples had tried other ways of meeting the difficulty, and had judged them even worse.

Whether or no we choose to criticise such customs, it is clear that they are directly comparable with letting people die of neglect in an affluent society today. The options are so different that the acts are simply not the same act, and very abstract talk about "absolute rights to life" or the like merely confuse us by obscuring the sheer size of this gap. We may think the Inuit were justified—or we may think that it is not possible for us to say whether they were justified—without thereby being committed to legitimating similar acts for ourselves. The cases are simply too different.

This is a positive reason for the judgement that we make. It is something totally different from a general sceptical belief that we cannot understand other cultures. And indeed, if we hear of this sort of thing being done in societies that are not under such severe pressure, then comparison begins to be possible again. We can then ask what the justification is, and can reasonably form opinions about whether it succeeds.

As I suggested earlier, there is nothing to stop us judging other societies validly across gaps of this kind, provided that we recognise that it is equally proper for the members of those societies to pass judgement on our own. We can, after all, grasp and allow for differences both of circumstances and of symbolism. Thus, in the case of the different ways of disposing of the dead we discussed in chapter 11, it makes sense for us to ask whether a Greek who ate his dead (or a Callatian who burned them) would have been doing wrong. We may well answer, "In general, yes, because, given the customs, this could not fail to be a calculated insult". The case is the same as for cannibalism in the West today. The existing symbolism is a fact of life and must be allowed for. And insulting others is in general wrong—even though special circumstances can sometimes excuse it.

WHAT DO WE DO ABOUT CONFLICT?

As far as its logic is concerned, disagreement is a much less desperate problem than many theorists seem to suggest. We are not in general much surprised by historical changes either in moral or factual views, nor by variation between cultures. Everywhere, we know that disagreement of both kinds is common. For both kinds, this disagreement can often be resolved by finding parts of the truth on both sides—always provided that somebody is prepared to take the trouble to look for them in a constructive and impartial way. And sometimes, with even greater efforts, it is possible to put the two halves of the truth together.

Much of the time people are not prepared to take this trouble. Often they are quite content to differ, and to assume that their own side is right without thinking much about it. But if they stop being content with this—if, for instance, some part of their own tradition begins to grate on them, or some part of a different one begins to impress them deeply—then they are quite capable of criticism, and of gradually changing their views. Once disagreement become perceptible at all, there is an obvious case for using that capacity. To assume offhand that those who differ from us are completely wrong—that they have no reason at all for taking the particular line that they do—seems foolish and baseless, equally over facts and values. Nobody should expect, in either area, to have a monopoly of the complete and final truth—to be immune against all future correction.

THE PLACE OF FEELING

There is, of course, a real difference in function between judgements of fact and value, one which does involve a reference to feeling. Though factual judgements too involve various feelings—for instance of confidence or hesitancy about belief—value-judgements typically call for a much wider range of feelings, and if they are moral judgements they carry also direct consequences for action. Propositions about the nature of carbon do not.

The important point, however, is that this presence of feeling does not imply the absence of thought. All judgements centre on thought, and any moral judgements that seem to involve no thought at all are exceptional and faulty. If, for instance, somebody just says baldly that a particular institution is wrong—playing football, say, or bigamy, or indeed marriage itself—without amplifying their ideas about it, then indeed we may say that this is just a feeling, just a subjective point of view. But that is saying that it is not really a judgement.

WHAT EXPLANATION DOES

In general, people can explain more fully what they mean, and it is this amplification, rather than any attempt at proof, that shows the presence of thought. The explanation makes it clearer *what kind* of fault or vice is in question—what is wrong about this particular institution. The objector to football might way, for instance, that there is too much aggression in football, or that large crowds are dangerous, or that the tribal hostility evoked is sinister, or that games are in some special way a waste of time. These are quite distinct kinds of objection. Until we know which of them is troubling the objector, we really do not understand (in a quite everyday sense) what the objection is.

The more fully these points are explained, the clearer the objection becomes. And, provided that the faults cited are serious moral faults, not just matters of taste, the more the objection begins to look like a genuine considered protest rather than just an expression of personal prejudice. When this happens, discussion can and does sometimes go on with great subtlety. People can begin to understand each others' point of view much better,

It is very important that the point of the discussion is explanation rather than proof. If somebody makes an unexpected value-judgement, the last thing that reasonable bystanders might be expected to say is "Prove it". Their more natural response is likely to be, "Oh but what do you mean?"

"Proof" is a term that belongs particularly to facts. It has accordingly got itself thoroughly entangled in Descartes' over-ambitious analysis of knowing, and has by now set itself such lofty standards that it is increasingly hard ever to use it with confidence. Thus, defenders of the tobacco industry still claim at times that there is "no proof" connecting smoking with lung-cancer, meaning that the entire causal chain has never been observed continuously. This continuous observation is something that has never been done for any causal connection beyond the shortest and most obvious. By this standard, very little of science is proved. And certainly such a standard has no relevance at all for moral truths.

"Proof" simply means "test", and the kind of test needed differs according to the function of the thing tested. When we are doubtful about a moral judgement, what we need is to have it more fully explained and the reasons for and against it more clearly stated. We may also need more time to think about it. But the idea of a proof—an argument that would neatly force us to accept it once for all—is senseless and irrelevant.

What explanation does is to specify. It does not just make a claim and emphasise it. It shows in detail *what kind* of recommendation that claim has. It makes sense of the feeling, rather than just expressing and defending it. And it functions both ways between positions, so that each respondent, by listening, finds out how to become more intelligible to the other.

EMOTIONAL DIFFICULTIES ARE REAL

This kind of mutual explanation is of course difficult for social reasons. Psychologically, it can often be a real marathon. Disagreement easily produces hostility, so that we merely want to shout at those who confront us and run away. But plainly, this is quite a different thing from a *logical* gap that would make reasoning impossible.

Hostility is just as common, and often just as strong, where the disagreement is on matters of fact. One might think of questions about the prospects for nuclear power, or about the relative intelligence of the different sexes or races, or about the effectiveness of capital punishment. Wherever the consequences are important, we hate to be opposed. That means that all such disputes are painful; they need to be handled with much more care than they usually get. But this is an entirely different thing from a logical obstacle blocking all reasoning.

WHAT KIND OF EXPLANATION?

It is interesting to notice how people in fact support, and expect others to support, moral judgements. Sometimes they are sure that no such support is necessary. What, for instance, demonstrates the Rights of Man? "We hold these truths to be self-evident", wrote Jefferson, Franklin, Tom Paine and the rest, laying down the American Declaration of Independence, and making claims that in many societies would have sounded most surprising. But they don't really depend on self-evidence, because they don't have to.

Although their Declaration was indeed epoch-making, these Founding Fathers did not have to strike out freshly into the void. They were not "inventing new values". They could rely on a background of argument already completed—on some most complex thoughts worked out, both in theory and in action, by their own age and by many before it. They could take for granted ideas about human liberty and equality forged by the Greeks, and also Christian views about the inestimable value of the individual soul. More immediately, too, they could rely on some negative attitudes—on hatred of tyranny, on a well-founded distrust of aristocratic institutions, on the fear of being oppressed.

In many cases, of course, there is no talk of self-evidence and very full arguments are given. But all moralists must rely also on an unspoken background—even those, like Sartre and Nietzsche, who are most eager to make an entirely fresh start. All put their points strongly and simply; all sometimes talk as if they were saying something totally new; all sometimes dogmatise. But they don't just innovate or dogmatise, and if they did they wouldn't have the influence that they have. If difficulties are raised, they need to be ready to explain more fully and subtly the points that they have put dramatically and simply. They must meet opposition, not just with blank denial and indignation (that is the role of fanatics) but with counter-argument and partial concession. And in doing this, they will have to connect what they say with values already familiar to their audience. They must deploy a whole imaginative vision that makes the point of what they are saying plain to their listeners or readers.

WHOLE AND HALF TRUTHS

Moral disagreement is hardly ever a simple confrontation between opponents who don't share each others' presuppositions at all. If they were as far apart as that, discussion would indeed be impossible. But then it would be so on factual questions as well. Normally a great deal is agreed, but is not mentioned, while the relatively small point of disagreement gets all the attention and all the publicity.

Our background of thought is a social network, a vast, complex web of assumptions into which we were born and within which we live. It is not our own private invention or creation, which we might desperately try to communicate to others. What we invent or create is a series of small changes within it, and we work on them co-operatively as members, not as quasi-divine legislators.

Normally, we move around inside this familiar, shared framework of moral beliefs at least as confidently as we do within our set of factual beliefs—which is, of course, also a shared one. There are always slight disagreements, indeed, the sense that this is so is an integral of our reassuring perception that other people are real. (A despot who can never find anybody to disagree with him is in a terrible situation, deprived of any normal social contact.) Most of the time we can live with disagreement without making serious changes. Sometimes, however, the disputes come to a head. There is conflict and discontent; there may have to be large changes. This is such a disturbing situation that we often perceive it as total blank opposition. Yet looking back at earlier changes, we can usually see that the various factions involved had a great deal in common, and that none of them was morally bankrupt; they all had some special moral insight to contribute. The difficulty was to drop tribal feeling sufficiently to fit them all together.

NOTES

The need for a common background if moral argument is to be possible has been well discussed by Michael Bavidge in another book in this series—*Mad or Bad?*

19

Back to the Main Question

Have we answered our original question? Can't we, after all, make moral judgements?

THE MORAL CASE AGAINST MORALS

We have been sorting out the difficulties about doing this supposedly sinister thing, and we have found many that were themselves moral objections. Some of these were not actually objections to judgement at all, but to practices that have often gone with certain ways of enforcing morality, such as vindictive punishment and indulgence in oppression. Others were objections to particular *ways* of judging—to bias, narrowness, chauvinism, lack of imagination, and willingness to limit individual freedom for the sake of Society.

But these objections too are moral ones, depending on particular judgements about values, notably about the sort of society we think we ought to have. The more we commit ourselves to these judgements, the less can we hope to move away from moral judgement altogether.

Yet in our time the individualistic moral bias that underlies these objections has been strong, and it has often been felt to be different from other biases—to arise from some new and legitimate way of judging, something different from the prejudices of the past. This is often expressed by claiming that it is aesthetic—merely a matter of taste and preference—not something accepted as a duty or an obligation.

The wish to escape from ideas of obligation is in general very strong. Ayn Rand's characters express it passionately. P.D. James' characters, similarly, are inclined to excuse the moral stands that they periodically take by saying that they just like acting in this way. And Baroness Wootton, had she been asked why, in the absence of any real moral values, she worked at penal reform, might well also have answered that that was just how she liked to spend her time.

This shyness about admitting obligations is quite understandable in view of frequent humbug in the past, but it is surely only a surface gesture. What we like to do depends a great deal on the world we have been brought up in and the values that we have accepted. One thing that we all undoubtedly like to do is to be acting in ways that are highly thought of—not only by others, but also by ourselves. We admire certain difficult styles of life, and honour people who manage to follow them. (This is as true, by the way, of the Mafia as of the saints; it is just that the ideals involved are different.) We certainly think, too, that we ourselves ought to do many things that we do not do, and also some things that we do do. And we sometimes do these things because we think we ought to. Why does the language of duty and obligation seem today embarrassingly unsuitable to express these obvious facts?

THE CELESTIAL OPTION

I have the impression that there may be here a certain humbug of individualism. We are unwilling to admit that we have not succeeded in organising for ourselves a totally enjoyable and fulfilling life. Doing things on principle strikes us as a rather drab and unfashionable activity, so we pretend to be doing them for enjoyment instead.

Like other kinds of humbug, this probably has certain advantages. It may well lead us to make more effort to enjoy what we must in any case do, which is certainly all to the good. But, as with other kinds of humbug, the pretence is unrealistic and confuses us. It is especially misleading when we are thinking about other people with hard duties—for instance, about those who have to care for aging relatives. It is much easier today than it has usually been before to say, "Oh well, that's what she likes doing". But this isn't any more true than it has even been.

The humbug lies in pretending that both the world and our own lives are now—in this modern age—so well designed that neither we nor anybody else has any obligation to do what they don't wish to. The pretence is produced by a wholly admirable attempt at producing the reality—at making the world paradisal. During the Enlightenment, there was a determined reversal of the fatalistic acceptance of suffering that earlier ages thought unavoidable. And this has indeed resulted in getting rid of a great deal of misery. But—the task proving far harder than was expected—further crops of the noxious stuff have sprung up all round us, and many of its central strongholds—notably in personal relationships—do not seem to have given way at all. Unhappily, unhappiness shows no sign of becoming obsolete.

What this means is that morality has not been put out of date in the simple way that has always looked so attractive—by making life so good that morals are not needed. Angels, it may reasonably be supposed, do not need a morality, because they never wish to do anything but what they ought to. In such a situation, duty and obligation lose their meaning. But that situation is not ours.

There is, however, a real point in attending to that imaginary situation, because it may lead us to recognise the great importance of feeling in morals. It really is far better to do what one ought *willingly*—feeling the need for it, seeing the point of it and throwing one's weight behind it—than to do it from the kind of "duty" that is totally reluctant and alienated, as is conveyed in the depressing phrase "a duty visit". If duty is merely the voice of the community—if nothing in ourselves accepts it, if our feelings do not respond to it—then, however good conduct may be, it is dead, and something absolutely central to morals is lost. On that point individualism is surely right.

EARTHLY OPTIONS: OTHER SPECIES, OTHER SOLUTIONS

Saying this, however, in no way helps us to get rid of morals. It merely adds one more requirement to them, asking us to make the effort to feel differently as well as to act differently. Though there are no doubt many cases where particular moral demands can be got rid of—where a more penetrating eye can show that they were artificial and unnecessary—these will only be a fraction of the moral scene. To get rid of all duties, we would have to stop being creatures prone to conflict.

Could we do that? It is worthwhile to consider for a moment the position of other social animals. Their lives are ruled by a very complex web of motivations, in which the acts that we think of as needing duty are often done by impulse. Many birds and mammals care for their young with impressive devotion, and also help and spare one another, not invariably, but to a striking extent. They also keep themselves clean, build what houses are necessary and sometimes hunt or forage co-operatively.

Plainly, this conduct does not result from prudent calculation and a social contract worked out between enlightened egoists. It springs from direct impulse, cumulatively building up into habit—at the individual level, from motivations arising out of neural states produced by evolution. They act as they want to, or (in bad times) as is least unwelcome in the circumstances. They do not have to be told not to be selfish. They are naturally fond of their young, and often of one another as well, and disposed to behave helpfully to them. (Incidentally, the notion that their genes *are* "selfish" in a quite peculiar and technical sense does not contradict this. It is merely a way of explaining how it has been possible for this other-regarding conduct to be developed in evolution.)

What, however, happens when two of these natural motivations conflict? Darwin noted an interesting case about the migration of swallows. He found that, when the fever for migration sets in—when flocks of swallows begin to gather and manoeuvre in the sky—those with late broods would without hesitation leave their young to die, even though, up until that moment, they had never ceased their strenuous efforts to feed them. This is fairly typical of the way in which one mood and one policy can at times succeed another for non-human animals. Sometimes there is no apparent conflict at all. Sometimes brief conflict can be seen, but there is no apparent upset to the later behaviour-pattern. These animals often seem able—as we are not—to shift from one policy to another that is quite at odds with it without any lasting disturbance.

HOW ARE HUMANS DIFFERENT?

This deep difference between human and non-human attitudes to the past and future is not often mentioned among the many things that are held to distinguish us from other animals. Yet it is surely of enormous interest. It does, no doubt, play some part in the "self-consciousness" which is often named as the main distinction here, but it is wider, because it is not solipsistic. It carries an awareness of *other people's* past and future selves as well.

We are, as Bishop Butler said, "plainly constituted such sort of creatures as to reflect upon our own nature". And as he put it more fully:

Brute creatures are impressed and actuated by various instincts and propensions; so also are we. But additional to this, we have a capacity for reflecting upon actions and characters, and making them an object of our thought; and on doing this, we naturally and unavoidably approve some actions, under the peculiar view of their being virtuous and of good desert; and disapprove others, as vicious and of ill-desert. That we have this moral approving and disapproving faculty, is certain from our experiencing it in ourselves, and recognising it in each other. It appears from our exercising it unavoidably, in the approbation and disapprobation even of feigned characters; from the words *right* and *wrong*, *odious* and *amiable*, *base* and *worthy*, with many others of like signification in all languages applied to actions and characters; from the many written systems of morals which suppose it... It is manifest great part of common language, and of common behaviour all over the world, is formed upon supposition of such a moral faculty, whether called conscience, moral reason, moral sense, or divine reason; *whether considered as a sentiment of the understanding or a perception of the heart, or, which seems the truth, as including both.*

(Bishop Butler, *Dissertation Upon the Nature of Virtue*)

Both Butler and Darwin noted it as a matter of plain fact that human beings everywhere pass moral judgement both on themselves and on each other, and that it is hard to see how anything like the kind of life that we think of as human could go on without this habit. In this ethological observation they were surely right.

ON HAVING A PAST AND A FUTURE

It is of special interest to notice how unavoidable it is that we should pass judgements on ourselves. Because we can look back and forward, we cannot help having some sense of our own identity through time. We therefore *own* the acts that we remember or contemplate as belonging to a continuing being—our "self". Because we see the future formation of that self as depending in some degree on our own choice, we cannot avoid thinking critically about it—distinguishing between better and worse aspects of it and possibilities for it. And because we live among others whose behaviour constantly affects us, and can recollect their past behaviour as well as our own, we are forced to think critically about them as well. (In fact, no doubt we begin to think about them long before we can think very clearly about ourselves.) To say that we are forced to think in this way is not to say that we come under any outside compulsion. It means simply that such thought is an inseparable condition of any coherent life and activity, because all coherence requires a self recognised as continuous.

Ought we, as has sometimes been suggested, to distrust this sense of our own continuing selfhood? Some philosophers (again, notably Hume) have applied systematic scepticism to the notion of personal identity, suggesting that we are really only successions of fleeting, momentary selves. There may be reasons for saying this within particular metaphysical systems. But it seems to be the kind of metaphysical doctrine that has little application at the level where we must live our lives—perhaps like rigid determinism, or indeed, like a belief that everything is radically a matter of chance. At the everyday level, we absolutely need to think of ourselves as continuous, even though we know that we continue through change. In saying this, we are not ignoring the prevalence of change. Our identity through time is that of organic things, comparable to that which makes acorn, seedling, sapling and adult oak count as a single tree, and makes spring, stream and adult Thames count as the same river. That kind of identity is quite enough to concern us deeply with the whole development, and to call for critical thinking about it.

PERCEPTIONS OF THE HEART

To call this thinking *critical* is not, or course, to suggest that it is a purely intellectual business. There can be no criticism without standards, which flow from solid, persistent, underlying emotional attitudes. At the end of the passage just quoted, Butler brings out with exceptional sharpness that the emotional and intellectual elements in this kind of thinking are inseparable. To have certain kinds of moral opinion simply *is* to have the corresponding feelings, and vice versa; the one cannot change without the other. Butler and Aristotle are almost alone among the great European philosophers in stressing this—in managing not to set up a cock-fight between Reason and Feeling, as if these were alternatives, or even separate people—as when Hume spoke of Reason as being "the slave of the passions".

PROBLEMS OF GUILT

What we have been and will be concerns us, and unavoidably—as Darwin pointed out—this brings in the possibility of guilt. The swallow may perhaps never remember the brood she has deserted. It would not be possible for a human parent not to remember it. Similarly, Jane Goodall reports that chimpanzees who have lost their tempers and whacked a dear friend violently, commonly show no sign whatever of remorse or apology, nor do their victims show indignation. Interestingly, what happens instead is that the victim, understandably upset, rushes to the aggressor with humble gestures of submission, begging to be taken into favour again. This the aggressor will usually do, and the episode ends with hugs and kisses all round—after which the friendship continues peaceably exactly as before. There is no judgement.

This can also happen with small human children of about two who have been shouted at sharply by a parent—but it is not long after that age before the child begins to be upset by the fact that it feels it has been attacked. It then cries, but does not approach the parent. It is, I think, making a judgement, though not necessarily a moral judgement. It thinks that something has gone wrong with the relationship. This chimps do not appear to do—so no judgement follows.

Because uncontrolled guilt and resentment can do such frightful harm in human life, it is not surprising that a nostalgic wish for some such arrangement plays a part in modern worries about morals. The price to be paid, however, would be heavy. Jane Goodall also notes the disturbing situation among the chimps when two somewhat abnormal females took to seizing and eating infants. Though the mothers of these particular infants fought desperately to save them, they got no help from the rest of the group. Nobody seemed to think it their business. No judgement was made. Again, a chimp who was crippled by polio was deserted and avoided by all, although he could pull himself around on his arms and was desperately seeking comfort from the others. Evidently, though personal relations among chimps are normally warm and friendly, there is something missing that we take so deeply for granted in human life that we

scarcely notice it—namely, a sense of continuity with the past, a rooted-
ness in earlier social contacts which can make it deeply shocking to murder
others or to desert a friend in difficulties. We should not, of course, forget
that human beings sometimes do these deeply shocking things too. But
that is something very different from never finding them shocking at all.

DOES HUMANITY NEED CONTINUITY?

This sense of continuity through time—this need to have some coherent
image of oneself and one's policy—is surely what accounts for the fact
that humans have been driven to develop morality, and have given it so
much prominence in their various cultures. If we ask what is the source of
the authority of morals, we are not looking outward for a sanction from
the rulers, or for a contract. We are looking inward for a *need*, for some
psychological fact about us that makes it deeply distressing to us to live
shapelessly, incoherently, discontinuously, meaninglessly—to live without standards.

That there must be such a fact seems clear from the proliferation of
moral principles, rules and ideals in our various cultures. These matters
get far more attention than would be needed merely for convenience—for
the mere traffic-rules required by prudence. Indeed these prudent traffic-
rules are often surprisingly neglected in favour of attention to ideals—to
the things that make life seem worth living rather than to those which
make it easier.

Why? "Your obligation to obey this law is its being the law of your
nature," said Butler. It is "an obligation the more near and intimate". And
although that metaphor of law is mysterious—although, too, we have
more difficulty than he noticed in deciding just what is the law of our
nature—that is indeed surely the role that we expect our morality to play.
We want it to be a set of principles that adjudicates the conflicts between
various demands, between the various parts of our nature, not just in a
way that eases the strain for the moment, but in one that we can live with,
that seems to point inward and forward towards the sort of life that will
satisfy our whole nature in the long run. Because our nature is social, this
life does not—as Ayn Rand and sometimes Nietzsche seem to have
thought—have to be one adjusted solely to our own wishes. But, because

we have so strong a sense of the past and future, it does have to be one that can last in principle.

Is this interest in continuity a weakness, or even a fault? Amoralistic writers have sometimes attacked it, reminding us that we ought not to be the slaves of our own past, any more than we should be the slaves of those around us or of Society. Plainly this is right in so far as it tells us not to be ossified. We must remain capable of change. But avoiding being ossified is not the same thing as having no backbone at all. A policy of total flexibility seems almost meaningless. If I adopt it today, what do I do tomorrow if I feel like committing myself to something again? My today's self could surely have no right to stop me from recommitting myself, since it has put up the flag for breaking the tyranny of past selves over present ones.

We certainly do have a choice about how stiff or flexible we will be—about how ready we are to make moral changes. But his is a matter of degree. In fast-changing times like the present, there are obviously reasons for not being too stiff about surface changes. But when we think about sticking to deeper principles—when, for instance, we hear about people who have resisted terrible pressures living under tyrannies—we surely see the advantages of stiffness exactly as our forefathers did.

Human life is constantly prone to throw up situations in which serving the ideals that one most deeply loves and chooses can demand immediate behaviour that one is going to hate. For instance, people in very many countries are often threatened with grim fates in order to make them betray their friends. If they resist, it is indeed possible to describe their behaviour by saying that they did what they really wanted, and many moralists have used this language. But there is something slightly wild and paradoxical about this way of talking, when in a perfectly obvious sense these people did what they were terrified to do, and did it because they thought they ought to.

NOTES

About the origins of morality, Darwin's views are of enormous interest. They are found in his *Descent of Man*, first edition, Volume 1 Chapter V, "On the Development of the Intellectual and Moral Faculties". (Other editions divide the chapters differently.) I have discussed these views in my book

Wickedness (London, Routledge, 1984) chapter 9, and have said something about the misleading effects of a superstitious, Lamarckian concept of evolution in my *Evolution as a Religion* (London, Methuen, 1985).

For Jane Goodall's observations of chimpanzees, see her *In the Shadow of Man* (London, Collins, 1971); and *Through a Window, Thirty Years with the Chimpanzees of Gombe* (Weidenfeld and Nicolson, London, 1990).

Works quoted in this chapter:

Bishop Butler, *Dissertation Upon the Nature of Virtue* (1726), section 1. Usually printed with his *Sermons* (my italics).

20

How Much Have Things Changed?

ARE MORAL DILEMMAS SOMETHING NEW?

People who suggest that something in the modern age has radically altered this situation, are, I think, often simply forgetting the great mass of fairly simple examples of this kind, and distracting themselves by deliberately looking only at specially chosen dilemmas, such as that of Sartre's student, which have been ingeniously constructed to appear insoluble. Both kinds of extreme case—the quite straightforward and the desperately puzzling—do occur, and have always occurred. But perhaps neither is very common.

In between them, there is a vast mass of moderate conflict cases which admit of some doubt, but a doubt which, given time and patience, may well be resolved—if not all at once, then gradually over a range of cases. The gradual erosion of savage revenge-codes during the history of many societies in favour of less savage legal systems is one example among many of how this is often done. On a more personal scale, the steady moral inventiveness of many individuals trying to grapple sensibly and humanely with a particular kind of situation—say divorce, or response to the insane, or the care of a handicapped child—can result in new ways of living that make previously insoluble dilemmas become soluble. It is because this can happen that we lie under some obligation to treat moral problems, even difficult ones, as soluble where possible, rather than fatalistically proclaim them hopeless.

EXTREMES ARE MISLEADING

Moral theory tends to treat the central mass of cases on one of the two extreme models. In the past, there has no doubt often been a bias to assimilating too many of them to the simple, straightforward model—to talking as if there were no conflicts, as if we all knew for certain what we ought to do. In the past century, however, there has been a reaction to the other extreme—to talking as if nobody ever knew what to do.

The peculiar, hypertrophied notion of "knowing", which we have noticed, lent force to this suggestion, and it is worth remarking again here that both these extremes of solubility are equally present on factual matters as well. There are plenty of unanswerable questions about facts. If one asks which investments will be doing best in a year's time, or what the weather will be then, or what the weather was on a particular day in the year 2,000 BC, or indeed who killed Olof Palme, one will not get an answer any quicker than Sartre's young man did.

This uncertainty extends also to practical but non-moral cases requiring judgement. Investors trying to choose between two rival investments may be baffled because the considerations on the two sides seem to have equal force. Was this perhaps what was troubling Sartre's young man too? Should we consider him as simply placed, like the donkey starving between the two equal bundles of hay, between two equally balanced courses?

In one way he is indeed like the donkey, in that altering the force of the two considerations eases his position. The donkey's difficulty is gone if he is moved slightly to one side, or if a little hay is removed from one bundle. Similarly, if the young man's mother becomes more independent, or if the war approaches his town, he may at once be able to choose.

Thus the point about equality of forces does matter, and in slight dilemmas it may be all that is troubling us. If we are hesitating interminably about what to wear this evening, we may recognise that and just toss up; all the rival clothes are quite adequate. In more serious cases, however, something else is wrong. What makes them painful—what, in fact, makes them moral choices—is that the two sides are not just equally balanced, they appeal to different sides of our nature. Choosing between them is favouring one part of oneself over another, and we stick because we are unwilling to commit ourselves to doing this.

Sartre has frozen his young man for us for ever in that state of deadlock, maintaining that nothing can be said to help him with it. Similarly Bernard Williams, in his book *Moral Luck,* has forcefully presented the case of Gauguin, hesitating whether to leave his family for his art, as an example of a dilemma which—Williams believes—in principle does not have an answer.

What does this amount to? The question "whether such dilemmas have answers" is of course not a factual one, like whether there is a pound coin under the cupboard. What we have here is a moral question about whether it is worthwhile to go on trying to think out an answer. Problems that have not been thought through so far may yet be so. If one is looking for a way of reconciling two claims—a way of at least doing more justice to both of them than has so far seemed possible—such a way can very often be found. And it will not, of course, be found if one has decided in advance that one is in a tragic bind where the two are in incurable competition.

Williams is rightly anxious, I think, to make a moral campaign for realism, both in admitting the harsh fact of competition where it does occur, and in not pretending that virtue always pays—not hoping that one will lose nothing if one does what is conventionally supposed to be one's duty. This realism is indeed vitally necessary. But it would not be so realistic to generalise this insistence into a bleak habit of accepting all dilemmas as final, because this paralyses further thought. Over time, our ancestors managed to rethink many customs—duelling and revenge for instance, and hanging people for sheep-stealing—in a way that showed a third path where there were formerly supposed to be inescapable dilemmas. And in a small way, people who constantly try to do this have their effect all the time in gradually altering customs.

How common, anyway, are insoluble dilemmas? There are indeed many problems that look insoluble at a first glance. But people—in both moral and non-moral cases—go on mulling these things until they often hit on some deciding consideration. Moreover, if a particular kind of dilemma becomes common, then more people tend to think and talk about it, so that deciding considerations become easier to find. In a habitually martial society, Sartre's young man would not have been half so mystified, because he would have been brought up among others who had faced that problem before him. His choice would still have been hard, but it would not have seemed totally incomprehensible.

MORAL DILEMMAS AND TRAGEDY

In fiction, the moment when things look most insoluble is of course often the one chosen for the story, and the plot may be deliberately devised so as to make them still harder. This is quite legitimate, both because such things do happen, and because they illuminate the nature of the choice that the writer wants to show us. Tragedy, though it is not the whole of life, and though there is a rather disagreeable form of humbug involved in pretending that one is tragically situated when one is not, is certainly of enormous significance.

Is there, however, something peculiarly and unavoidably tragic about our situation today? This is quite widely held, but I doubt that it does justice to the struggles of people in earlier ages. The difference that is often held to exist between the modern predicament and earlier ones is sometimes brought out by saying that (for instance) Hamlet is a modern hero but Macbeth is not. The distinction is that Macbeth "knows" that what he is planning is wrong—he hasn't the slightest doubt of it—while Hamlet is utterly unsure about that very thing. Macbeth operates within a single, unquestioned moral code, while Hamlet is caught between two codes—a simple revenge-ethic and a more sensitive, human system in which you simply do not kill people, especially members of your family, in cold blood. Thus (the argument goes on) Macbeth's question about what he ought to do had a quite simple answer, whereas Hamlet's had no answer. Hamlet's predicament is therefore the more deeply tragic, but it is also the one to which we are all condemned now that past moral certainties have vanished for ever.

What should we make of this distinction?

It is undoubtedly a quite interesting division between two kinds of tragedy. But this division is surely not one of date or epoch; it is between two kinds of central character, both of which exist at all times. Very roughly, it is between the kind of person who thinks about moral questions and the kind who doesn't. It is quite true that Macbeth sees the question of whether to murder Duncan in black and white terms. For him, the act is simply wrong:

> He's here in double trust;
> First, as I am his kinsman, and his subject,
> Strong both against the deed; then as his host,

Who should against his murderer shut the door,
Not bear the knife myself. Besides, this Duncan
Hath borne his faculties so meek, hath been
So clear in his great office,...
    I have no spur
To prick the sides of my intent, but only
Vaulting ambition, which o'erleaps itself
And falls on the other

(Act I, scene vii)

At this point, he has almost talked himself into giving up the scheme, but this reversal is far too weak to resist his wife's contempt when he names it to her. She does not have to argue. What was Macbeth's intent at the beginning of the scene is still his intent at the end. Essentially, he sees his problem at this point simply as one of making up his mind to do this wrong thing. That seems to him a fairly straightforward project though he finds it difficult. In wishing for "a spur" he is surely hankering for a grievance—a provocation from Duncan that would rouse him and get him over the difficulties that his unbridled imagination keeps raising. Failing that, what he wants is someone else to make his mind up for him—as the witches roused him to it in the first place—and he readily accepts this service from his wife.

They both see the decision as an isolated one—a necessary step in their upward progress, like moving house or buying some new armour—something that can afterwards be forgotten. The extent to which they have misunderstood themselves—and therefore their whole situation—in supposing this is what constitutes the tragedy. They thought of the moral aspect of their act as a simple, given, limited thing which could be put in its place in their plans and shovelled aside without loss. But they find they are mistaken.

To point this out is not to be sentimental or moralistic. It is not to say that crime never pays. It is simply to notice that morality tends to be much more pervasive and often deeper-rooted than it looks. Hamlet, who is well aware of this for a start, would not be likely to fall into so simple a snare, and accordingly the one he faces is indeed far more complex. He does not know what he ought to do, and neither, indeed, do we. He has reason to say:

The time is out of joint, O cursed spite
That ever I was born to set it right

(Act I, scene v)

This is a thought that would never occur to Macbeth.

OLDER DILEMMAS

Does this, however, mean that Hamlet's tragedy is of an especially modern kind? Scarcely. Nearly twenty-five centuries ago, at the very beginning of European tragedy, Aeschylus treated the similar dilemma of Orestes, who must decide whether to kill his mother because she has murdered his father. Aeschylus' *Oresteia* is quite explicitly written as an attempt to grapple with the large-scale clash of moral systems that Orestes' predicament raises. Similarly the *Bhagavad Gita*, which was written a century or so earlier, opens with Arjuna's impassioned appeal to Krishna to tell him what on earth he is to do to avoid the war that is being forced on him by his uncles, who are invading his kingdom:

> Krishna, though they should slay me, yet would I not slay them, not for the dominion over the three worlds, how much less for the earth alone!... Even if, bereft of sense by greed, they cannot see that to ruin a family is wickedness and to break one's word a crime, how should we not be wise enough to shun this evil thing?... Are we really bent on committing a monstrous evil deed, intent as we are on slaughtering our own folk because we lust for the sweets of sovereignty? O let the sons of Dritarashtra, arms in hand, slay me in battle, though I, unarmed myself, will offer no defence; therein were greater happiness for me.

Krishna, however, warns him that there is no way out this way; refusing to act is still acting. We are in the world and have to play our part in it.

In both these tragic situations, the fact that the dilemma is unavoidable is the starting-point of the action. In both, no evasion is possible. The terrible act must indeed be done. What the writers then do, however, is to grapple with the meaning of it. They use it for a starting-point towards a whole new way of viewing the world.

In the *Oresteia*, Athene and Apollo take part, helping the humans to struggle towards a state of things in which revenge-systems give way to a more equitable kind of justice. The blood-feud, seemingly interminable, is ended. By their advice, too, the deep, primitive emotions that called for revenge are not insulted, but find their place in the human heart acknowledged. There emerges a different interpretation of what it is to be a human being—a harmony with others less corporate and mechanical, more free and intelligible. In the *Bhagavad Gita*, Krishna tells Arjuna how he must go forward, past the wise and balanced statesmanship that has been his ideal so far, to a kind of detachment in which he can do those terrible acts that are really required of him, but without falling into the terrible motives that would normally accompany them. This, of course, calls for a much wider change—for an understanding of the sense in which all earthly things are illusion, and an apprehension of the deeper reality which underlies them. It calls for enlightenment.

These are metaphysical solutions—that is, they concern the background presuppositions of thought, the inclusive worldview within which detailed questions are contained. They are only two among a great number that are possible. Since this is not a book on metaphysics, I cannot deal with them very fully here. I can only point out how naturally they arise from any serious thought about these dilemmas, and how much larger is their scope than might have been expected. They are not failed attempts to answer the question, "what can this particular hero do now that will avoid evil?" They accept that he has a choice of evils. But they go on to reflect on what such a choice means, and on the place of evil in the whole cosmos.

IS METAPHYSICS A LUXURY?

There are those who suppose that such solutions have now become impossible, because, as Auguste Comte suggested, all metaphysics is obsolete, having been only a mistaken fantasy belonging to the childhood of the human race—a mere set of unnecessary assumptions used in the process of abandoning the infantile comfort of religion. This is a muddle. Metaphysics is not something you can get rid of; it is a necessary condition of all extended thought. To have a metaphysic is to have a conceptual structure underlying one's world picture, a general map of how the world is and how it can possibly be. Metaphysical doctrines include obviously necessary things like views about causal necessity, such as determinism and indeterminism; views about the reality of physical objects and the possibility of knowledge, about the proper way to think about mind and matter, time and space, and—of most interest to most of us—views about human nature and human destiny. They are the most general presuppositions of our thought, without which it would remain a hopelessly shapeless collection of scraps. Comte and his followers had their own peculiar metaphysics; they did not have none at all.

Those of a Comtian persuasion might be tempted that what is said in the *Oresteia* and the *Bhagavad Gita* must be obsolete because it involves gods. This would be superficial. In fact, in both poems, the gods are there simply as counsellors. They are not arbiters coming down in machines to perform miracles or to impose a ready-made solution; they are personifications of wisdom. They too are beings inside the whole, not in charge of it, and their contribution concerns the right way to think about that whole.

It is, however, of course no accident that they are divine. Human beings trying to widen their horizons, to find a context adequate for the consideration of difficult dilemmas, very commonly do invoke a divine dimension. The results vary in quality from the highest to the lowest of human achievements, and there seems little doubt that Comte was being childish in assigning them all to the childhood of the race—if indeed the race ever had a childhood.

Comte's attempt was part of a campaign, very characteristic of the "modern" age, to make metaphysics more economical—to believe in as little as possible apart from the things we actually experience. Though some of these economies certainly have been worth making, the campaign suffers from two grave drawbacks.

One is humbug—pretentiousness about the actual range of our experience. This experience is so scrappy that very wide assumptions going far beyond it are quite unavoidable; the only thing gained by professing economy is that you don't know you are making them. There have been, in modern times, quite a number of supposedly economical metaphysical systems—for instance those of Hume, Marx, Nietzsche, Freud, Sartre and Ayer. It has gradually become plain that they do not achieve economy, because what they are trying to do cannot be done simply. They are often of baroque complexity, and contain extraordinary dogmas.

The second drawback is false economy—the loss of necessary elements from thought. Saving belief is like saving money, it is not an end in itself; it is a means to wise expenditure. I can easily cut down my range of beliefs by becoming a solipsist, thus ceasing to believe that other people are conscious. Or I could become a phenomenalist, thus ceasing to believe that material objects exist when I am not there. But to do this would not be economy, it would be a wild kind of miserliness. The right question to ask about apparently extravagant metaphysical views is, what is their function? what are they achieving? They are there to provide the background which makes other thinking, and thereby other action, possible. When we are confronted with tragic dilemmas, that is what we need. And what we have to ask about metaphysical systems is: do they do this for us?

Sometimes, of course, the thinking is not directly metaphysical; what is provided is simply a new imaginative vision that gradually changes our view of things at the everyday level. This is typically what Shakespeare does. If one were asked whether there is any moral in Hamlet, it would of course be crude to say that the play is a tract against the concept of revenge. It is not. But it is about revenge. It is a study of what it is like to be dragged up to a case of it and have to live it through. The effect of doing this—as Shakespeare did it again and again—is humanising, civilising, it stirs the imagination, it makes it possible to look directly at customs instead of merely treating them in stereotype. If this works, it can gradually bring it about that situations of this kind are avoided. Though this will never mean that there are no more tragic dilemmas, it is surely again. What tragedy does, then, is not to show that moral thinking is impossible but to stir it up, to cause more of it.

NOTES

About moral dilemmas, and especially about Bernard Williams' treatment of them, I have said something more in *Wickedness*, chapter 2, with a fuller discussion of the meaning of immoralism.

ENVOI

Throughout this little book, I have been suggesting that, far from being helpless in the matter of thinking morally, we have considerable powers for doing that very difficult thing. If this is so, it seems to be somewhat wasteful to entertain confused taboos and inhibitions that stop us doing it. To name a parallel, it is worthwhile remembering the fate of the Margrave of Brandenburg. He seems not to have bothered to look at his post, and therefore he never opened a particular parcel of music that had been sent to him as a present by some tiresome choirmaster. It was found unopened at this death.

The choirmaster's name was J.S. Bach, and the parcel contained what we now call the six Brandenburg Concertos. Not much else is known about the Margrave. No doubt he was a man who got a lot of presents. All the same, it seems possible that he, like the rest of us, sometimes reflected that life was hard on him, and that he had never had the luck that he deserved. It does not seem to have occurred to him that he could have improved the situation just by opening his mail.

It would surely be a great pity if we were to repeat this mistake in regard to that very remarkable gift, our power of making moral judgements.

INDEX OF PROPER NAMES